Sophie McKay's Quick Guide on Companion Planting

Sophie McKay's Quick Guide on Companion Planting

A Practical Guide to Smart Plant Pairings of Vegetables, Fruits, Herbs, and Flowers for a Thriving, Pest-Free Garden

Written by Sophie McKay
www.SophieMcKay.com

Copyright © 2025 Sophie McKay

Published in the United States of America, 2025

Legal Notice: This book is copyright protected. This book is only for personal use. All rights reserved. No portion of this book may be reproduced, stored in a retrieval system, or transmitted in any form or by any means – electronic, mechanical, photocopy, recording, or any other – except for brief quotations in a book review, without the prior written permission of the author or publisher. For more information, contact www.sophiemckay.com

First edition, 2025
ISBN 978-1-916662-37-7 (paperback)
ISBN 978-1-916662-38-4 (ebook)
ISBN 978-1-916662-39-1 (hardback)

Website: www.SophieMcKay.com
Email: Sophie@sophiemckay.com
Author page: https://www.facebook.com/Sophie.McKay.Author
Facebook: www.facebook.com/groups/garden.to.table.tribe

Table of content

Table of content 5
INTRODUCTION 9
CHAPTER 1 The Secret Language of Plants 11
The Fundamentals of Companion Planting 11
What is Companion Planting? 11
Key Concepts and Terminologies 15
Regional Considerations: Companion Planting for Different Climates 19
Practical Tips and Plant Examples for Climate-Specific Gardening 20
Understanding Your Garden's Microclimates 23
Sun Chart 24
Choosing Microclimates for Different Plants 25
Garden Planning 25
Garden Mapping 25
Garden Zones 26

CHAPTER 3 Soil, Water, and Space Considerations 30
The Foundation of Growth: Companion Planting and Soil Health 30
Soil Types and Their Characteristics 32
Enhancing Your Soil with Amendments 36
Homemade Fertilizers 41
Water Management: Nurturing Your Garden Sustainably 43
Rainwater Harvesting: Maximizing Natural Resources 44
Tips for Maximizing Rainwater Collection 45
How do swales work? 46
Drought-Resistant Gardening 47

Maximizing Small Spaces with Companion Planting . 49
Container gardening 51
Raised beds...53
Building Your Raised Bed Oasis: Tips & Tricks 54
Maximizing Yields with Succession Planting 57
Your Own Planting Calendar..59
Intercropping Fast and Slow-Growing Crops 59

CHAPTER 4 Companion Pairings & Cheat Sheets............62
Vegetable Companion Planting Guide 64
Companion Planting Guide for Fruits 77
The Magic of Herbs 89
Companion Planting Guide for Herbs 90
Pest Repelling Herbs.. 101
The Role of Flowers in Companion Planting 104
Companion Planting Guide for Flowers 106
Interesting mixes... 112

CHAPTER 5 Troubleshooting and Common Pitfalls 117
Signs Of Trouble 118
How to Work Around Allelopathy in Companion
Planting 118
Common Allelopathic Plants 119
Eco-Friendly Pest Management Strategies 121
Keeping Your Garden Healthy: Understanding
Integrated Pest Management (IPM)............................ 123
Organic Methods of Pest Control 125
Integrating Pollinator-Friendly Practices 127
Adapting Your Garden for Seasonal Changes 129

Conclusion 131

Quick guide for beginner's favorites 133

Companion Plants for Vegetables 1. 134

Companion Plants for Vegetables 2. 135

Companion Plants for Fruits 1. 136

Companion Plants for Fruits 2. 137

Companion Plants for Fruits 3. 138

Sun Map 142

Please Leave a Review! 143

Unlock the Secrets to Thriving Fruit Tree Gardens! 145

If You Liked This Book, Try This One Too! 146

Welcome to Permaculture! 147

Bibliography 148

Looking for a gardening companion?

This Garden Planner is the perfect choice.

This guide is your trusty companion for planning, tracking, and celebrating the life in your garden, ensuring you enjoy every step of your gardening journey. Inside this logbook, you'll discover:

- **Dream Garden Planner**: Define your ideal garden and make it a reality.
- **Comprehensive Inventories**: Keep track of your **tools, seeds, roots, bulbs, shopping lists, and expenses**.
- **Seasonal Chore Planners**: Stay on top of your gardening tasks in every season, from early spring through to winter.
- **Garden Layout and Sun Map**: Plan your garden strategically.

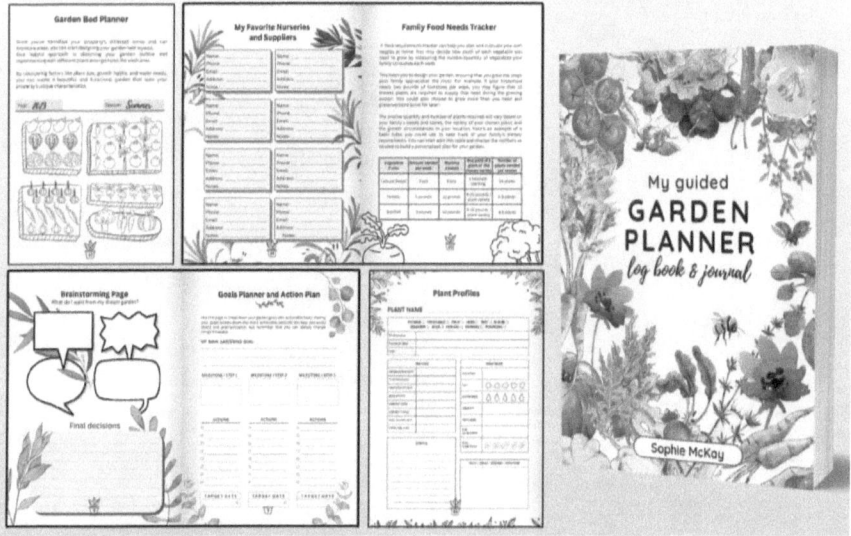

- **Planting Timelines and Health Tracking**: Get insights on when to sow and harvest while **keeping an eye on rainfall, pests, and diseases**.
- **Pollinator Fan Page**: Celebrate the vibrant and your garden's ecosystem.
- **Tips&Tricks:** Dive deeper into gardening with **Square-Foot Gardening basics, a Companion Planting guide, the grow-bag cheat sheet** and more.

Just scan this QR code with your phone or visit the https://Gardenplanner.SophieMckay.com link to land directly on the book's Amazon page.

INTRODUCTION

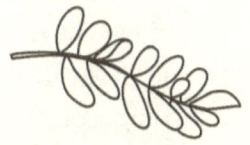

Growing up on my grandparents' farm, I couldn't imagine living without green spaces. Flowers bloomed in our garden all year round, and we always had fresh vegetables to eat. Living in that environment, gardening became second nature to me. Then, as a young college student, I moved to my first apartment in the heart of the city.

Imagine a garden where plants thrive naturally, fighting off pests and replenishing the soil with nutrients all on their own. Picture bountiful harvests, bright-colored fruits, and vegetables making their way to your kitchen — all without the use of chemicals. This is the power of companion planting. Dating back centuries, this clever technique has long been used by gardeners to create thriving and self-sustaining ecosystems. When you combine this powerful technique with an understanding of your local weather conditions and microclimate, you can enjoy abundant harvests throughout the year, even during the coldest seasons.

My previous works—"The Practical Permaculture Project," "The Ultimate Guide to Raised Bed Gardening," "The Beginner's Guide to Container Gardening," and "How to Grow Fruit Trees Fast and Easy"—explored practical, actionable advice to increase harvest, cut down costs, and strengthen plant health. In this book, I've condensed my knowledge into an easy-to-follow format focused on companion planting. This guide is crafted for both beginners and seasoned gardeners eager to adopt sustainable, chemical-free practices that deliver outstanding results.

Each chapter is full of practical tips, step-by-step instructions, detailed guides, and troubleshooting tips to help you overcome common gardening challenges. You'll find plenty of budget-friendly, DIY solutions and sustainable practices that you can put into action right away. You will also find a compact list at the end of the book, which you can use as a quick resource.

With this book as your guide, you'll be well on your way to creating a beautiful and thriving garden. This guide will walk you through the essentials of companion planting, explaining how plant relationships works and why biodiversity is key to a healthy garden. You'll learn how to design a garden plan that maximizes space, conserves resources, and suits your local climate. It also includes companion pairings for vegetables, fruits, herbs, and flowers, with detailed charts and explanations to help you make the best choices. Along the way, you'll find practical tips on soil preparation, watering, pest control, and seasonal care, plus troubleshooting advice to tackle common challenges and keep your garden thriving year-round.

By the end of this guide, you'll have the knowledge and tools to create a garden that is not only beautiful but also productive, sustainable, and full of life.

Let's dive in!

CHAPTER 1

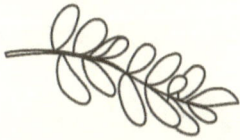

The Secret Language of Plants

The Fundamentals of Companion Planting

Have you ever noticed how some plants just seem to click when planted together? It's like they're best friends, helping each other grow! This magic is called companion planting, and it's all based on some pretty cool science. Let's decode this secret language and learn what your plants are talking about.

What is Companion Planting?

Believe it or not, plants are always talking to each other, even if we can't hear them. They send secret messages to each other using different chemicals. Some plants send messages like "Stay away!" but others are more friendly, encouraging others to "Come closer" so they can help each other out. Companion planting is about understanding all these connections: who helps whom, who shares what, and who needs a little shade. It's like creating a self-sustaining ecosystem right in your backyard. And the best part? It's a natural way to garden, so you don't need to use harsh chemicals. It's good for your plants, good for the environment, and good for you!

One way plants help each other is by sharing nutrients. Legumes, like peas and beans, trap nitrogen from the air and add it to the soil. The plants growing in the vicinity of these nitrogen factories benefit from the enriched soil and flourish as a result. Come to think of it, it's a lot like sharing a delicious meal with your neighbors!

The benefits of companion planting extend from the garden to our dinner table. Certain plant combinations give rise to more flavorful food. For example, when grown together, tomatoes and basil produce more flavorful varieties. Basil not only makes tomatoes taste better but keeps pesky bugs away. Carrots and onions are another winning combination. The onions keep the carrot flies at bay while the carrots grow vertically, allowing the onions more room underground. Similarly, beans and corn help each other thrive. The corn gives the beans a support structure to climb on, like a built-in ladder. Meanwhile, the beans enrich the soil with nutrients for the corn to feast on. Other great examples of companion planting are marigolds and tomatoes. The marigolds act like tiny bodyguards, keeping nasty bugs away from the tomatoes so they can grow big and juicy.

Understanding the secret language of plants helps us create a super healthy garden where plants share resources and help each other in all sorts of ways.

Let's check out the main benefits of companion planting:

- ***Optimizing Growth and Yields*** - Companion planting can significantly impact plant growth and yields. Some pairings enhance nutrient uptake, while others provide physical support or shade. For example, the "Three Sisters" method, a traditional Indigenous practice, combines corn, beans, and squash. The corn provides a trellis for the beans, the beans fix nitrogen in the soil, and the squash's broad leaves create shade and deter pests.

- ***Enhancing Flavor*** - Certain companion plants can enhance the flavor of nearby crops. For instance, basil is known to improve the taste of tomatoes when planted together.

- *Improving Soil Health* - A healthy soil is the foundation of a thriving garden. Companion planting contributes to soil health in several ways. For example, deep-rooted plants help break up compacted soil, improving water and nutrient absorption for shallow-rooted companions. Legumes, like clover or beans, fix nitrogen, enriching the soil naturally. Deep-rooted plants can access nutrients in lower soil layers and bring them closer to the surface, benefiting shallow-rooted companions.

- *Boosting Biodiversity and Natural Pest Deterrence* - Companion planting promotes greater biodiversity in the garden, increasing resilience against pests and diseases. A diverse plant community attracts beneficial insects that help control pest populations naturally, reducing the need for chemical interventions. For example, marigolds deter nematodes and attract ladybugs, which help manage aphid populations.

- *Continuous Harvest* - Interplanting fast-growing crops with slower-maturing ones ensures a continuous supply of fresh produce. This strategy allows for staggered harvesting, maximizing productivity throughout the growing season.

- *Space Optimization* - Pairing plants with different growth rates frees up garden space. Combining tall, sun-loving plants with shorter, shade-tolerant ones create a layered arrangement, allowing multiple plant species to thrive in close proximity. For instance, climbing beans planted alongside corn enable the beans to grow vertically without additional stakes. Similarly, low-growing herbs or leafy greens beneath taller plants help suppress weeds, retain soil moisture, and maximize garden space.

- *Softening microclimate effects* - Tall plants, such as sunflowers or corn, act as natural sunshades, protecting smaller, sun-sensitive plants like lettuce or spinach from harsh sunlight. By creating a shaded microclimate, these taller companions prevent delicate plants from overheating and wilting under the intense sun, much like giving them a little umbrella on a scorching day. Furthermore, these taller plants can also act as windbreaks, protecting more vulnerable plants from strong gusts. This manipulation of the immediate environment, through strategic plant placement, allows gardeners to create a more balanced and favorable growing space, enabling a wider variety of plants to thrive together.

Benefits of Companion Planting

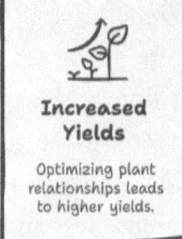

Increased Yields

Optimizing plant relationships leads to higher yields.

Reduced Chemical Use

Natural pest deterrents reduce reliance on chemicals.

Improved Flavor

Certain plants enhance the flavor of their companions.

Efficient Use of Space

Companion planting maximizes garden space and resources.

While the right plant combinations can work wonders, environmental conditions and their placement in the garden also plays a significant role. This includes weather patterns in your region, the specific microclimates in your garden (a sunny corner versus a shady spot), and soil type. For example, some plants thrive in sandy soil, while others prefer clay. Even the specific varieties of plants you choose make a huge difference. For instance, a particular tomato variety might be more susceptible to certain pests, regardless of its companion plants.

Meticulous observation and record-keeping are essential for successful companion planting. Keeping a garden journal will allow you to track your plants' progress, document your observations, and analyze the results. (See the appendix for sample journal pages and templates, including plant variety trackers, companion pairing logs, and garden mapping tools.) Start small with only a few simple pairings, such as zucchini and dill or carrots and onions. Observe how the plants interact with each other, document your findings, and gradually expand your companion planting efforts. This approach minimizes being overwhelmed and allows you to learn through experience, building a solid foundation for future success.

Key Concepts and Terminologies

Gardening has a language of its own. The different terms and concepts might seem a bit overwhelming at first but understanding them is key to truly unlocking the power of companion planting. So, let's explore some of the most important terms together and make sure you're ready to speak fluent garden!

Allelopathy

Allelopathy refers to the chemical influence plants have on each other. Some plants release chemical compounds in the soil that inhibit the growth of nearby species. For example, black walnut trees secrete juglone, which can stunt or kill sensitive plants. It's important to consider these plant relationships when planning your garden layout.

Beneficial Companions

There are plants that support each other. Certain plant pairings work synergistically, where one plant's presence enhances the growth, flavor, or pest resistance of another. Tomatoes and basil are a classic example of this phenomenon.

Biodiversity Planting

Growing lots of different plant species together is known as biodiversity planting. The practice creates a more resilient ecosystem. Greater biodiversity helps manage pests, diseases, and soil fertility. It prevents a single species from taking over garden resources, reduces vulnerability to environmental stresses, and boosts overall garden health.

Dynamic Accumulators

Plants with deep or extensive root systems that draw nutrients from the subsoil are known as dynamic accumulators. When these plants are used as green manure (chopped and dropped), they release their stored nutrients back into the topsoil.

Guilds (Guild Planting)

Imagine a fruit tree surrounded by a team of helpful plants—some attracting pollinators like bees, others keeping the soil healthy, and some helping to suppress weeds, almost like a support group for your fruit tree. This is known as guild planting, a permaculture method that mimics natural ecosystems by grouping together compatible plants. The guild centers around a key plant, like a fruit tree, with different companion plants growing nearby, chosen for their specific roles, such as nitrogen fixation, nutrient accumulation, or pest control. For example, you might plant clover (a nitrogen fixer) and borage (which attracts pollinators) around an apple tree.

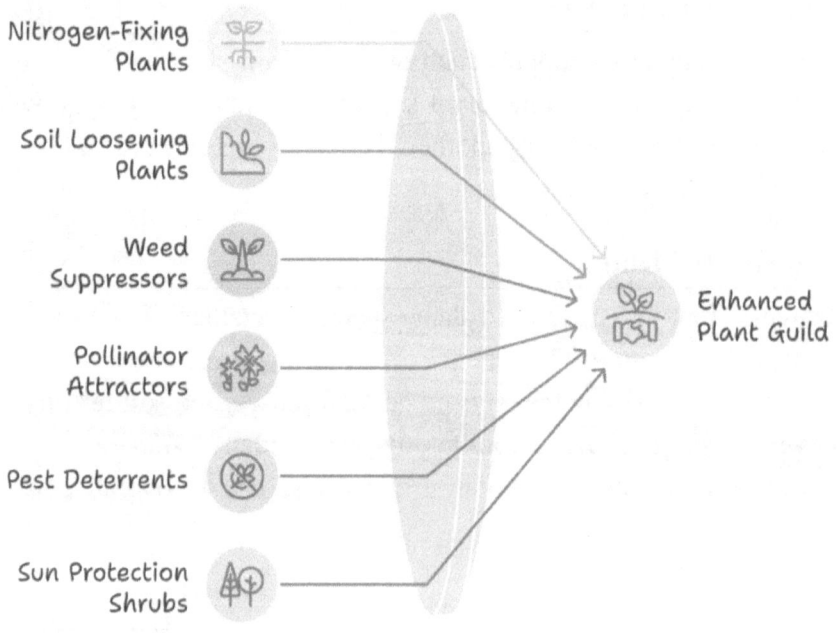

Intercropping

This involves growing two or more crops in close proximity, often in alternating rows or mixed together. Intercropping maximizes space utilization, optimizes resource use, and disrupts pest invasions. For example, intercropping legumes with cereals can improve soil fertility as the legumes fix nitrogen.

Living Mulch

Instead of using traditional mulch materials, living mulches use low-growing ground cover plants, like clover. This helps suppress weeds, retain soil moisture, and enrich the soil with organic matter as the tiny cover plants decompose.

Mutualism

This describes a symbiotic relationship where both (or all) partners benefit. The classic "Three Sisters" planting method (corn, beans, and squash) is a great example of mutualism: the corn provides support for the beans, the beans fix nitrogen for the corn, and the squash provides ground cover.

Nitrogen Fixation

This is a natural process carried out by certain bacteria, often in partnership with leguminous plants. They convert atmospheric nitrogen into a form that plants can use, enriching the soil and reducing the need for synthetic nitrogen fertilizers.

Permaculture

Permaculture is a holistic gardening practice that goes beyond just companion planting. It encompasses a wide range of sustainable practices, including polyculture (growing many different plants together) and guild formation (creating plant communities that support each other, like the fruit tree example we discussed), to create self-sustaining and regenerative ecosystems. The goal is to design gardens and landscapes that work in harmony with nature, minimizing our reliance on external inputs like fertilizers and pesticides. I've discussed these techniques and more in my previous book, The Practical Permaculture Project. Make sure to check it out to learn more about this amazing gardening practice.

Polyculture

Polyculture is the practice of growing multiple crop species together in the same space at the same time. It mimics the diversity of natural ecosystems, increasing resilience to pests and diseases, improving soil fertility, and often leading to more stable yields compared to monocultures (growing a single crop). Plants in this system interact with each other by sharing nutrients and deterring pests.

Relay Planting

This involves growing a new crop in the same spot before the previous one is harvested. For instance, sowing bush beans between rows of maturing spinach. By the time the beans mature, it's time to harvest the spinach.

Repellent Plants

These plants naturally deter pests. Some examples include marigolds, renowned for their ability to repel nematodes and aphids.

Trap Cropping

This technique involves planting a less valuable "trap" crop to attract pests away from your main crops. The trap crop acts as a diversion, preventing insects from damaging your more desirable plants and reducing the need for pesticides.

Grasping the key terminology of gardening is like learning the language of your plants. It allows you to truly understand their needs and how they interact with each other. Now that you're familiar with these essential terms and concepts, you can approach your garden with confidence, ready to explore the myriad possibilities that companion planting offers. You'll also be able to actively join any gardening conversation, sharing tips and experiences with fellow enthusiasts using the same vocabulary!

Up next, we'll explore garden designing and planning. So grab a paper and pen, and get ready to sketch the garden of your dreams!

CHAPTER 2

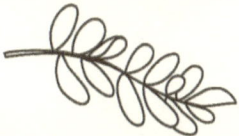

Designing Your Garden Plan

It's time to set up your garden! But before you get in the car and drive to your nearest gardening center, pause and look at the weather and check your location. Depending on your region, you may encounter different challenges while companion planting. For example, environmental factors like cold, harsh winters, or lack of rainfall can limit the kinds of plants you can grow. To navigate these environmental challenges, it's essential to understand your climate zone and plant accordingly. For instance, if you live in an arid climate, look into drought-tolerant varieties. If the place where you live gets a lot of snowfall, check out frost-resistant plants.

Regional Considerations: Companion Planting for Different Climates

In North America, the USDA Plant Hardiness Zone Map is the standard. It divides the continent into 13 zones based on average annual minimum winter temperatures. Knowing your zone is crucial because it helps you identify the plants that will most likely survive and thrive in your area. You can find your USDA zone on the official USDA website: https://planthardiness.ars.usda.gov/. Alternatively, you can search online with the following: "[Your City] USDA zone" (e.g., "London USDA zone").

While the USDA zones are predominantly used in North America, similar systems exist in other regions. In Canada, the Plant Hardiness Zones are also based on minimum winter temperatures, in addition to other factors like maximum temperatures, rainfall, and snow cover. Zone systems in Europe tend to vary. They're often based on average minimum winter temperatures, but there's no single, universally adopted standard like the USDA zones. Australia uses a similar system based on minimum temperatures along with other climatic factors. This is why I think it's best to search "[Your Country] plant hardiness zone" to find the most accurate information and choose your plants accordingly.

Practical Tips and Plant Examples for Climate-Specific Gardening

Let's look at some tips and tricks to make your plants flourish in different gardening zones:

Dry/Arid Zones

e.g., USDA Zones 8-10, Mediterranean Climates

Practical Tips:
- Try mulching for moisture retention. A layer of organic mulch not only conserves water but keeps the soil temperature consistent, reducing stress on plants.
- Consider using drip irrigation to deliver water directly to plant roots, minimizing evaporation.
- Choose native plants, as they are often well-adapted to local conditions.
- Consider using water wise landscaping methods.

Plant Examples:
- Pair lavender with drought-tolerant succulents. Lavender's aromatic oils deter pests, while succulents offer a unique texture and visual appeal, creating a garden that is as functional as it is beautiful.
- Plant rosemary alongside sage and thyme. These herbs not only tolerate dry conditions but enhance each other's flavor and deter pests.

- Pair artichokes with oregano. Artichokes are drought tolerant, and oregano can help to repel pests.
- Pair olives with capers. Both thrive in hot, dry conditions and rocky soil.
- Plant drought-resistant prickly pear cactus with native desert wildflowers to help fight long-dry spells.

Cool/Northern Zones

e.g., USDA Zones 3-6, Canadian Prairies, Scandinavian Climates

Practical Tips:
- Use row covers or cold frames to protect tender seedlings from unexpected frosts, giving them a head start in spring.
- Plant in raised beds with insulated sides to extend the growing season and prevent soil freezing.
- Consider using dark mulches to absorb heat from the sun.
- Use greenhouses or polytunnels to extend your growing season.

Plant Examples:
- Focus on root vegetables and cold-hardy greens.
- Consider planting kale with garlic. Kale's frost-resistant leaves provide greens throughout winter, while garlic offers natural pest control.
- Pair cabbage with dill. Cabbage likes the cold while dill repels cabbage moths.
- Plant spinach with peas. Cold, hardy spinach grows best with nitrogen-fixing peas.
- Pair rhubarb with horseradish. Both are incredibly hardy and tolerate cold, wet conditions.
- Plant blueberries with cranberries. Both thrive in acidic soil and cold climates.

Temperate Zones

e.g., USDA Zones 7, UK, Parts of Australia

Practical Tips:
- Take advantage of the early spring and late fall growing seasons by planting cool-weather crops like lettuce, spinach, kale, and radishes before and after summer.
- In summer, focus on heat-loving crops like tomatoes, peppers, squash, and beans.
- Avoid planting the same family of crops in the same spot each year to reduce pest buildup and nutrient depletion. Follow a rotation plan: Leafy greens → Legumes (beans/peas) → Root crops (carrots, beets) → Fruit crops (tomatoes, squash)

Plant Examples:
- Pair tomatoes with basil. This is a classic example of companion planting. Tomatoes thrive in the sun, and basil repels pests and enhances the flavor of tomatoes.
- Plant lettuce with strawberries. Lettuce likes the shade from the strawberries, which in turn repel pests.
- Pair beans with corn. Try the classic three sisters method by adding squash.
- Plant roses with garlic. The garlic wards off aphids, protecting the roses.

By understanding your climate zone and adapting your companion planting strategies, you can create a thriving and productive garden. Start using a Seed Starting and Planting calculator, which will help you to select the perfect seed starting times, based on YOUR local average frost dates! You can download one for free from my website, form www.sophiemckay.com/free-resources.

Now that we've explored the different climate zones, let's scale down and analyze the different microclimates in our garden.

Understanding Your Garden's Microclimates

Imagine stepping into your garden on a crisp morning. Pay attention as you wander through your garden, and you might experience subtle changes in different areas. One corner might feel sunny and warm while another remains cool and shaded. These variations are known as microclimates – small areas within your garden where conditions differ from the surrounding environment. Understanding them allows you to choose the best possible locations for your plants.

Microclimates arise from factors like your garden's orientation, nearby structures, trees, and even the materials used in your landscape. A south-facing wall, for instance, will absorb and radiate more heat, creating a warmer microclimate suitable for sun-loving plants. Conversely, areas shaded by trees or buildings tend to remain cool, ideal for shade-tolerant species. Although small, these variations can significantly impact plant growth.

Benefits of growing plants in their preferred microclimates - Use the hidden microclimates in the nooks and crannies of your garden to your advantage. Here are some benefits of doing so:

- **Extended Growing Season** - Warmer microclimates allow you to plant earlier in spring and harvest later in fall.
- **Optimized Plant Placement** - You can match plants with their ideal growing conditions, leading to higher yields.
- **Increased Plant Diversity** - You can cultivate a wider range of plants, including those that don't commonly grow in your climate.
- **Reduced Plant Stress** - Cooler microclimates provide refuge for heat-sensitive plants, protecting them from stress and potential damage.

Observation is the first step to identifying the different microclimates in your garden. Pay attention to how sunlight moves across your garden throughout the day and year. Note which areas receive the most light and warmth. South-facing walls are excellent for heat-loving plants like tomatoes and peppers. Shaded areas are perfect for leafy greens like lettuce and spinach. Even fences and hedges create microclimates by blocking wind or casting shade. You'll be amazed by your garden's hidden potential.

And now, let's go outside!

1. Take a walk through your garden with a notebook and pen.
2. Observe and record different areas, noting sun exposure, temperature variations, and structures that influence these conditions.
3. Sketch a simple map of your garden, marking the microclimates you identify.

To better understand sun exposure, you can create a simple sun chart. It's a simple exercise that can reveal a number of hidden treasures in your garden!

Sun Chart

Observe your garden at different times of the day (morning, midday, afternoon) and note the areas that receive direct sunlight, partial shade, or full shade. Do this throughout the seasons as the sun's angle changes. This visual record helps you map your garden's microclimates.

Zone	Time			
	9 AM	11 AM	2 PM	6 PM
West wall	Shade	Partial sun	Very hot - full sun	Full sun
Vegetable garden	Partial sun	Sun	Sun	Sun
Apple tree area	Shade	Shade	Partial sun	Shade
South fence	Sun	Sun	Partial sun	Shade
Fireplace	Shade	Shade	Sunny - often windy	Sunny

Choosing Microclimates for Different Plants

When choosing plants, consider their light, temperature, and water requirements. For example:

- **Sunny, Dry Microclimates** - Succulents, drought-tolerant herbs like rosemary, thyme, and lavender, and vegetables like tomatoes and peppers.
- **Shady, Moist Microclimates** - Ferns, hostas, leafy greens like lettuce and spinach, and shade-loving flowers like impatiens.
- **Windy Microclimates** - Hardy shrubs, wind-resistant herbs like sage, and plants with strong root systems.
- **Warm, Sheltered Microclimates** - Heat-loving plants like basil, peppers, and eggplants.

Garden Planning

Deciding where to grow and what to grow are two crucial questions that can make or break a garden. Coming up with the best possible garden layout is a slow process, requiring a lot of thought. Mapping out the space based on environmental factors and dividing the area into zones can help us make the best decisions

The goal is to group similar plants together. This will make gardening a whole lot easier. For starters, it simplifies watering. When you have similar plants grouped together, you don't have to worry about over or under-watering. This makes it easier for you to focus on other areas, such as spotting potential problems like pests or nutrient deficiencies. Plus, it helps you use your resources more efficiently.

Garden Mapping

As discussed before, we must consider factors like sunlight, water access, and plant spacing as we map out our garden. A well-planned layout ensures that each plant has the space and resources it needs to thrive. Below is a step-by-step guide to garden mapping, which is the first step to creating garden zones.

Step-by-Step Guide to Garden Mapping:

1. **Sketch Your Layout** - Draw a map of your garden, marking the spots where you want to place different plants, trees, and shrubs (consider the mature size of each plant and leave enough space for growth).
2. **Check out your sun map** - Which spots are the sunniest? Where are the shady corners? Color the shady and sunny areas on your map.
3. **Group Plants by Needs** - Create some lists. Group together plants with similar water and sunlight requirements to simplify maintenance.
4. **Plan for Pathways** - Include clear paths between garden beds to facilitate movement and maintenance.

The above steps will help you determine the best locations for your plants. For instance, a sunny, well-drained area near your kitchen door might be perfect for a herb spiral bed whose unique design not only maximizes space but creates diverse microclimates within a small area, allowing you to grow a variety of herbs with different needs.

Garden Zones

Imagine dividing your garden into distinct "rooms," each with its own purpose. This is garden zoning, and it's all about grouping plants with similar needs together. Here are some zones you should consider for your garden

Kitchen Garden (Zone 1)

- **Location** - Closest to your home for easy access.
- **Contents** - Herbs (basil, thyme, parsley, sage) and quick-harvest vegetables (lettuce, radishes).
- **Benefits** - Convenient harvesting for cooking.

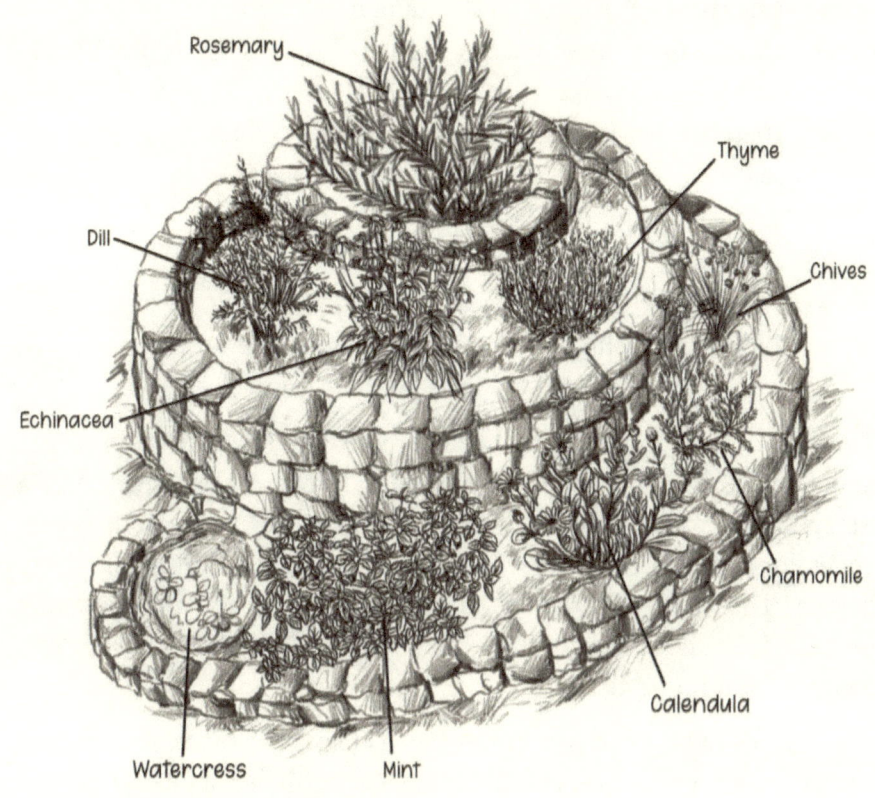

Vegetable & Flower Beds (Zone 2)

- **Location** - Adjacent to the kitchen garden.
- **Contents** - Vegetables with longer growing seasons (tomatoes, peppers, carrots) and flowers (marigolds, zinnias).
- **Design** - Organize beds for crop rotation and companion planting.

Fruit Zone (Zone 3)

- **Location** - Further from the house.
- **Contents** - Berry bushes and dwarf fruit trees.
- **Considerations** - Ensure adequate spacing and sunlight for fruit production.

Perennial Edibles (Zone 4)

- **Location** - Perimeter of the garden.
- **Contents** - Perennial vegetables (asparagus, rhubarb) and herbs.
- **Benefits** - Minimal maintenance and yields over multiple seasons.

Composting Area (Zone 5)

- **Location** - Discreet, accessible corner.
- **Purpose** - Collect kitchen and garden waste for compost.

The benefits of zoning extend beyond mere convenience. It simplifies maintenance routines by allowing you to focus on one section at a time. For example, when it's time to water, you can concentrate on the zones that need it most rather than dragging a hose throughout the garden. This focused approach also makes it easier to spot potential problems, such as pest infestations or nutrient deficiencies, and address them promptly.

Zoning aids in targeted pest control measures. By isolating plants that attract certain pests, you can implement specific strategies to protect them without affecting other zones. For instance, you might use natural deterrents like garlic spray in a vegetable zone prone to aphid attacks while leaving the herb zone undisturbed.

When you're planning your garden, remember that flexibility is key. Gardens are living, changing spaces. As seasons shift and plants grow, you might need to adjust your layout. Don't be afraid to experiment and try new things. Use a garden planner to map out your zones, track plant progress, and note any seasonal changes. It will also help you decide when to plant, care for, and harvest your crops. You can find sample journal pages in the appendix to get you started.

Companion planting is a lot like matchmaking for your plants. Garden mapping and planning allow you to identify the best locations for your plants, taking out the guesswork from the equation. With the tips above, you'll have a clear roadmap for your planting decisions. And the best part is that you can personalize your gardening space so that it reflects your personality. Because a garden is more than just a place to grow food; it's an extension of you. So, personalize your plan! Do you love cooking? Create a dedicated herb garden. Are you passionate about butterflies? Plant nectar-rich flowers to attract the beautiful, winged creatures. Let your imagination soar and create a garden that reflects your unique tastes and preferences.

In the next chapter, we'll delve into the foundational aspects of soil, water management, and garden bed types and learn how these planting essentials work together to create a flourishing garden.

CHAPTER 3

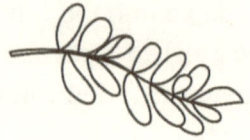

Soil, Water, and Space Considerations

The success of your garden hinges on three factors: soil, water, and space. Getting them right can make all the difference for your plants. So, let's take a closer look at these gardening essentials and their impact on plant growth.

The Foundation of Growth: Companion Planting and Soil Health

A thriving garden begins with healthy soil. It's more than just dirt under your feet; it's a dynamic ecosystem teeming with life, crucial for plant growth and overall garden productivity. Understanding your soil's condition is essential. A simple soil test can reveal its pH and nutrient levels, providing a baseline for improvement.

Soil structure is equally important. It influences water retention, root penetration, and overall plant health. Deep-rooted plants like radishes and carrots naturally aerate the soil as they grow, breaking up compaction and improving drainage. This aeration prevents waterlogging and root rot, creating channels that facilitate better root growth for other plants. This natural process is far more sustainable than mechanical methods and helps maintain the soil's integrity.

Companion planting plays a vital role in nurturing your garden's ecosystem. One of its most significant contributions is nitrogen fixation. Certain plants, primarily legumes like beans and peas, form a symbiotic relationship with bacteria in their root nodules. These bacteria convert atmospheric nitrogen into a usable form for plants, enriching the soil naturally. This reduces the need for synthetic nitrogen fertilizers, promoting a more sustainable approach. Pairing nitrogen-fixing plants with nitrogen-hungry crops, such as tomatoes or corn, creates a balanced nutrient cycle, leading to healthier plants and increased yields.

In addition to the above, organic matter also plays a crucial role in maintaining a healthy soil. As plants grow and decompose, they contribute valuable organic material, improving soil texture and fertility. Companion planting accelerates this process by ensuring a continuous cycle of growth and decay. For instance, leafy greens like lettuce or spinach, used as ground cover, quickly decompose, adding organic matter and supporting beneficial microorganisms. This diverse range of plant residues contributes various nutrients, fostering a rich and balanced soil environment.

Living mulches, such as clover, offer another innovative approach to soil health. Unlike traditional mulches, living mulches are low-growing plants that cover the soil surface. They suppress weeds, conserve moisture, reduce erosion, and contribute organic matter as they decompose. Clover, in particular, also fixes nitrogen, providing a dual benefit. Planting living mulch creates a dynamic, self-sustaining ecosystem where each plant plays an important role in the garden's overall health and productivity.

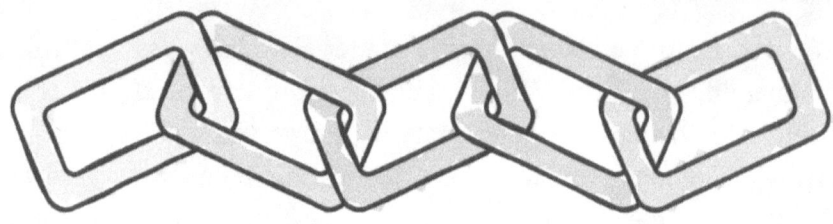

Enhancing Soil Health Through Plant Interactions

Nutrient Availability	Soil Structure	Organic Matter	Living Mulches	Soil Testing
Plants enrich soil with essential nutrients	Deep roots improve drainage and prevent compaction	Decomposing plants add vital organic material	Low-growing plants suppress weeds and conserve moisture	Kits provide insights into soil composition and needs

Soil Types and Their Characteristics

Each soil type has its own set of characteristics, influencing water retention, drainage, and nutrient availability. Once you've performed a soil test in your garden, it's time to decipher the results. Whether your soil turns out to be sandy, clayey, loamy, or a combination of these, you can make the most of it by selecting the best-suited plants and making soil amendments. So, let's look at the different soil types and their properties.

1. Sandy Soil

Sandy soil feels gritty to the touch and drains water quickly. It warms up rapidly in the spring, which can be beneficial, but it also tends to dry out and lose nutrients easily. Adding organic matter is crucial to improve water retention in sandy soils.

Plants that like it:

- **Herbs** - Lavender (especially Lavandula angustifolia 'Hidcote' or 'Munstead'), rosemary (Rosmarinus officinalis 'Prostratus' or 'Arp'), Thyme (Thymus vulgaris or creeping thyme varieties)

- **Vegetables** - Carrots (*Imperator* or *Nantes* types), Radishes (*Cherry Belle* or *French Breakfast*), Melons (cantaloupe or watermelon), Asparagus
- **Flowers** - Sunflowers (Mammoth or Dwarf Sunflower varieties), Yarrow (*Achillea millefolium*), Gaillardia (Blanket Flower), Coreopsis (Tickseed), Echinacea (Coneflower - also tolerates clay)
- **Other** - Yucca, Sedum

2. Silty Soil

Silty soil has a smooth, almost soapy texture. It retains moisture and nutrients well, but it can become compacted. Adding organic matter is essential to improve drainage and prevent compaction.

Plants that like it:

- **Vegetables** - Beans (Bush or Pole varieties), peas (Sugar Snap or English peas), Corn (Sweet Corn varieties), Cucumbers, Squash
- **Ornamental Grasses** - Most varieties, including Feather Reed Grass (*Calamagrostis x acutiflora 'Karl Foerster'*), Switchgrass (*Panicum virgatum*), Little Bluestem (*Schizachyrium scoparium*)
- **Flowers** - Hydrangeas (especially *Hydrangea macrophylla*), Astilbe, Hostas (also tolerate clay), Coneflowers (also tolerate clay), Ligularia
- **Trees & Shrubs** - Willows, Dogwoods, Red Twig Dogwood

3. Clay Soil

Clay soil feels heavy and sticky when wet and becomes hard when dry. It retains water well, but poor drainage can lead to waterlogging. Clay soil is also slow to warm up in the spring. Adding organic matter and gypsum can improve drainage and structure.

Plants that like it:

- **Flowers** - Hostas (especially *Hosta sieboldiana 'Elegans'* or *Hosta 'Sum and Substance'*), Coneflowers (especially

Echinacea purpurea), Daylilies (especially *Hemerocallis fulva* or double varieties), Black-Eyed Susans (especially *Rudbeckia hirta*), Bee Balm (especially *Monarda didyma*), Asters (especially *Symphyotrichum novae-angliae* or *Symphyotrichum cordifolium*), Clematis (especially *Clematis viticella varieties*)
- **Vegetables** - Brassicas (cabbage, broccoli, cauliflower, kale), Brussels sprouts, Leeks
- **Trees & Shrubs** - Oak trees, Maple trees, Viburnums, Forsythia, Serviceberry

4. Loamy Soil

Loamy soil is considered the ideal soil type. It's a balanced mix of sand, silt, and clay, offering good drainage, water retention, and nutrient availability. Adding organic matter to this soil type can help maintain its balanced state.

Plants that like it:

- Almost everything! Loam is the gardener's best friend. Just be sure to choose varieties suited to your climate and growing zone.

5. Peat Soil

High in organic matter, acidic, and retains moisture well. Often found in bogs and wetlands.

Plants that like it:

- **Acid-loving plants** - Azaleas, Rhododendrons, Blueberries (*Highbush* or *Rabbiteye* types), Camellias
- **Other** - Heathers, Cranberries, Pitcher Plants, Sundews

Believe it or not, creating your own soil is not difficult at all, and the process is extremely gratifying. Knowing the exact contents of the soil gives you more control over satisfying your plant's unique requirements.

Usually, a good potting mix recipe contains a mix of sterile garden loam, peat moss, sand, and other additives. Let's look at some proven recipes for preparing container soil adapted from Planet Natural Research Center.

Classic Soil-Based Mix

Peat moss or mature compost	1 part
Garden loam or topsoil	1 part
Clean builder's sand or perlite	1 part

The organic material in the recipe above provides structure, while the sand improves drainage. You can also add a balanced, slow-release fertilizer for more benefits.

Soil Mix for Raised Beds and Large Containers

The following recipe is for 4 ft by 8 ft (1.25 x 2.5 m) raised beds / large containers that are one foot (30 cm) deep.

Black Gold Peat Moss	5 bags (11 cubic feet or 300 l)
Teufel's Organic Compost	4 bags (4 cubic feet or 110 l)
Worm castings	4 bags (4 cubic feet or 110 l)
Organic chicken manure	3 bags (3 cubic feet or 80 l)
Therm-O-Rock Vermiculite	2 bags (4 cubic feet or 110 l)
Azomite	3 - 6 lbs (1.5 - 2.5 Kg)
Kelp meal	1 - 2 lbs (0.5 - 1 Kg)
Oyster shell flour	3 - 6 lbs (1.5 - 2.5 Kg)
All-purpose fertilizer	2 - 4 lbs (1 - 1.8 Kg)

Spread a large tarp on the ground and mix all the ingredients on it before you start filling the beds. This will prevent the formation of pockets of peat, manure, or other ingredients and keeps the mess contained. If the amounts sound too big, simply use the given proportions with smaller quantities.

Enhancing Your Soil with Amendments

After identifying your soil type, you can use amendments to improve its characteristics and create a more favorable growing environment. Soil amendments are materials added to the soil to improve its physical or chemical properties.

Healthy soil is the cornerstone of productive gardening, and soil amendments are your tools for making this foundation stronger. Incorporating the right amendments helps you balance nutrients for robust and healthy plants. A well-amended soil also improves structure, ensuring proper aeration and drainage, which are vital for root development.

One of the most effective ways to do this is through composting. It involves transforming kitchen scraps and garden waste into nutrient-rich compost, a natural fertilizer that enhances soil health. You can choose between hot composting, which rapidly breaks down materials through high temperatures, and vermicomposting, which uses worms to produce nutrient-dense compost. Both methods create rich humus that improves soil texture and fertility, fostering a healthy environment for plants.

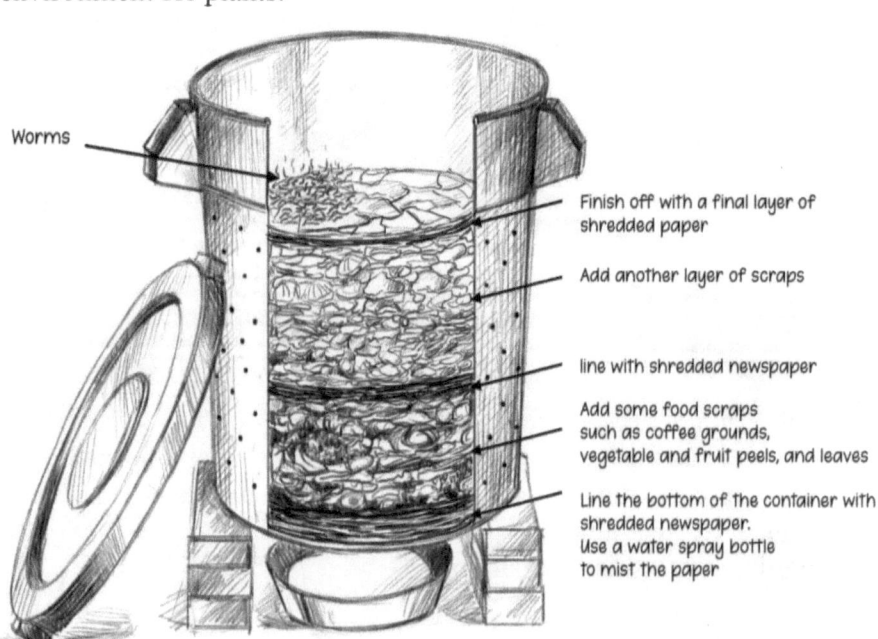

But how does composting work? Think of it as turning your kitchen scraps and yard waste into super-powered garden food. It's as simple as allowing nature to do its thing—breaking down stuff like banana peels, leaves, and even old cardboard into rich, fertile soil.

Creating a compost system is a pretty straightforward process. All you need is a good spot for your compost pile or bin, some place with good air circulation and drainage. Once you've found the perfect spot, it's time to gather materials like vegetable scraps, coffee grounds, and dried leaves and start layering! Layer these in a bin, alternating between 'green' stuff — like those fruit and veggie scraps and fresh grass — with 'brown' stuff, like dry leaves and cardboard, to keep things balanced.

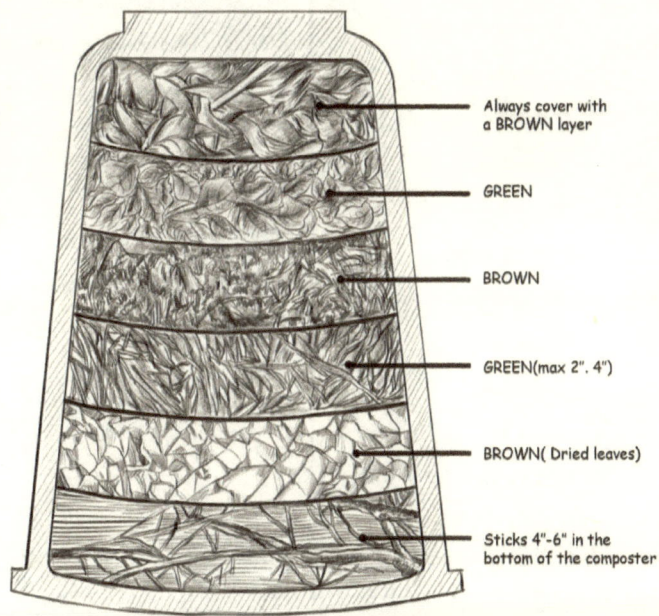

Turn the layers every few weeks to aerate and speed up decomposition. For hot composting, aim for a balance of green (nitrogen-rich) and brown (carbon-rich) materials, maintaining a temperature that encourages rapid breakdown. Vermicomposting will require a bin with bedding material — shredded paper or leaves — and red worms, which efficiently process organic waste into valuable compost. Both methods result in a dark, crumbly product that's ideal for enriching garden soil.

Here's a chart to help you decide what's considered 'green' and 'brown.' Have a look to get an idea of the materials you'll need.

It's best to aim for a ratio of 3:1; i.e., 3 parts brown materials (carbon-rich) to 1 part green materials (nitrogen-rich) by volume. This ensures a good balance of carbon and nitrogen, which is essential for healthy compost.

You'll also need to keep the layers a bit damp and give it a good turn every now and then to let the air in. After a while, all those little worms will turn your pile into dark, crumbly compost that's perfect for your garden. Composting not only makes your plants happy but keeps the trash out of landfills, making it a win-win for your garden and the environment.

You also can use compost tea to provide your plants with the micronutrients they need, along with fortifying beneficial microbial populations in the soil. Here's a simple recipe for making compost tea:

Compost Tea

1. Put 2 cups of well-rotted compost or worm castings in a 3-gallon (10 liter) bucket of water.
2. Stir well, allowing it to stand overnight.
3. Stir again after 12 hours, letting the particles settle.
4. Pour the mixture into containers, using the remaining sludge for another batch or adding it directly to another container.

Nettle Tea

1. Collect nettle by pulling it out by the roots or using scissors or shears to cut it.
2. Fill a bin with nettle, cutting its into smaller pieces.
3. Add water to the bucket and give it a stir.
4. Place a lid on top of the bucket, but ensure adequate airflow.
5. Allow the mixture to decompose for a month.
6. Stir whenever you observe bubbles on the surface.
7. Wait for one to two weeks for the nettle tea to be ready.
8. Strain the liquid when its ready (the mixture will stop bubbling after stirring), separating solids from the liquid.
9. Dilute the resulting black liquid and add to the soil of your plants.
10. Use within 6 months.

In addition to composting, you can also try mulching to enhance your soil's quality. The technique uses organic materials like straw or wood chips that are layered on top of the soil, conserving moisture, suppressing weeds, and slowly adding nutrients as they break down.

By using soil amendments, we can boost our garden produce and improve the quality of our harvest. These amendments can either be organic or inorganic. Here's a quick round-up of both types:

Organic Amendments

Organic amendments are derived from living matter. They improve soil structure, water retention, and nutrient availability and feed beneficial soil organisms.

- **Compost:**
  Compost is decomposed organic matter that adds nutrients, improves soil structure, and boosts beneficial microbial activity. It's good for all soil types and can be added anytime to boost soil fertility. Add it regularly, especially before planting and as a top dressing.
- **Manure:**
  Manure is rich in nutrients, but it should be well-rotted to avoid burning plants. It improves soil structure and fertility and is best for nutrient-poor soils. Add it in the fall or early spring, allowing time for decomposition.
- **Peat Moss/Coco Coir:**
  Peat moss or coco coir improves water retention and aeration, particularly in sandy soils. It also adds organic matter and helps with soil acidity. Add it when planting or when soil water retention is poor.
- **Leaf Mold:**
  Leaf mold, made from decomposed leaves, is excellent for adding organic matter. It improves soil structure and water retention and is great for all soil types. Use it as a mulch or mix it into the soil.

Mineral Amendments

Mineral amendments are inorganic materials that alter soil pH or improve drainage. They provide specific nutrients and improve the physical properties of the soil.

- **Lime**
  Lime raises soil pH (makes it more alkaline) and is essential for plants that prefer alkaline soil. Add it based on soil test results if the pH is too acidic. Lime should be applied in the fall, allowing time for it to integrate before spring planting.

- **Sulfur**
  Sulfur lowers soil pH (makes it more acidic) and is essential for plants that prefer acidic soil. Add it based on soil test results if the pH is too alkaline.
- **Gypsum**
  Gypsum improves clay soil structure and adds calcium. It helps with drainage in clay soils. Add it when dealing with compacted clay soils.
- **Perlite/Vermiculite**
  Perlite and vermiculite improve drainage and aeration. They're good for container gardening and heavy soils. Add them when planting or when drainage is poor.

It's important to spread the amendments evenly and work them into the top few inches of soil for best results, ensuring they reach plant roots effectively.

Homemade Fertilizers

Different plant types require different fertilizers. Regardless of the kind of fertilizer you choose, it should be composed of the following elements:

1. Nitrogen (N): Stimulates stem and leaf growth
2. Phosphate (P): Strengthens root growth.
3. Potassium (K): Promotes flower and fruit production.

For instance, leafy plants like spinach require plenty of nitrogen, as do tomatoes and peppers during the start of the season for developing strong stems and leaves. Later in the season, tomatoes need large quantities of potassium for fruit production. Commercially available all-purpose fertilizer contains a balanced concentration of each of the three major elements, making it an all-around satisfactory fertilizer.

If you want to provide your plants the nutrition they require without splurging on store-bought fertilizer, here are four homemade recipes you can try.

1. **Epsom Salt Fertilizer**

Epsom salt	1 tablespoon
Water	1 gallon (3.7 liter)

Mix and shake well. Apply the solution to your plants once a month during the growing season. Epsom salt provides plants with magnesium and sulfate, making it an excellent fertilizer for magnesium loving plants such as peppers, roses, tomatoes, and potatoes.

2. **Used Coffee Grounds**

Place a newspaper on a cookie sheet and spread your used coffee grounds, letting them dry completely for a few days. Mix the dried-up coffee grounds with the soil of your acid-loving plants that require nitrogen, magnesium, and potassium. They will slightly shift the soil pH toward acidic, which will benefit plants such as blueberries, rhododendrons, roses and azaleas.

3. **Fish Water**

Simply pour old water from the fish tank into your garden beds or containers instead of pouring it down the drain. Fish tank water is teeming with nitrogen and other nutrients necessary for plant growth.

4. **Broken Eggshells**

Save broken egg shells, letting them air dry and grinding them into a fine powder. Add this powder to your plant containers as a natural substitute for lime. The calcium carbonate present in the eggshells makes the soil pH slightly more alkaline, leading to better absorption of nitrogen, phosphorus, and potassium by the plants.

Mixing the eggshells with vinegar causes a reaction between acetic acid and calcium carbonate, making the calcium more bioavailable for the plants. Combining your broken eggshells and vinegar fertilizer techniques can be very powerful.

Another great way to improve particularly challenging garden soil is by using raised beds. They allow you to create a customized growing medium using a blend of topsoil, compost, and other amendments. This gives you greater control over soil conditions regardless of your native soil type. Raised beds also improve drainage and can extend the growing season. We will discuss the benefits of raised beds and how to build them in the next part of this chapter.

Water Management: Nurturing Your Garden Sustainably

Water is the lifeblood of your garden. In an era of climate change and increasingly unpredictable weather patterns, conserving water is more important than ever. Efficient water use not only preserves this precious resource but reduces waste, keeping your garden both environmentally friendly and cost-effective. As gardeners, we must adapt to the changes in the environment, ensuring that our plants receive the moisture they need without depleting our water supply. This involves rethinking traditional watering practices and embracing techniques that maximize every drop.

One of the most effective strategies to reduce water use is implementing drip irrigation systems or soaker hoses. These systems deliver water directly to the plant's base, minimizing evaporation and ensuring that moisture reaches the roots where it's needed most. Unlike traditional sprinklers, which can waste water through runoff and evaporation, drip irrigation offers precision watering, making it ideal for both small gardens and larger plots. This method not only conserves water but promotes healthy plant growth by providing consistent moisture levels, reducing the risk of disease caused by overwatering.

Mulching, which we discussed above, is also a great way to enhance water retention. A layer of organic mulch, such as straw, shredded leaves, or wood chips, acts as a protective barrier, reducing evaporation from the soil surface and maintaining even moisture levels. It also suppresses weed growth, so your plants have an abundant supply of water and nutrients. By keeping the soil cool and moist, mulch creates an optimal environment for root development, fostering robust growth. This simple technique also improves soil health over time.

Rainwater Harvesting: Maximizing Natural Resources

Rainwater harvesting is another excellent way to make the most of natural resources. By collecting rainwater, you can reduce your reliance on municipal water supplies and provide your garden with fresh, untreated water. Consider these easy methods to collect rainwater:

Use Rain Barrels

- Position barrels beneath downspouts to capture rainwater from your roof, then use this water to irrigate your garden during dry spells.
- Ensure the barrels are covered to prevent mosquito breeding.
- Use a spigot to easily access the collected water for irrigation.

Create Rain Gardens

- Create a dedicated area that will collect rainwater runoff from your roof or driveway.
- Plant this area with plants that can handle periods of both wet and dry soil conditions.

Which plants will thrive in your rain garden?

- **Switchgrass** (Panicum virgatum) - A native grass that thrives in a range of soil conditions, from wet to dry, and is drought-tolerant once established.

- **Black-Eyed Susan** (Rudbeckia hirta) - This hardy perennial can handle both moist and dry soils and is known for its bright yellow flowers.
- **Daylilies** (Hemerocallis spp.) - These resilient plants tolerate a wide range of soil moisture levels and are low-maintenance.
- **Joe-Pye Weed** (Eutrochium purpureum) - A native perennial that can grow in wet soil but adapts to drier conditions once established.
- **Sedum** (Stonecrop) - Succulents like sedum are drought-tolerant but can also handle occasional wet soil, making them ideal for variable conditions.
- **Iris species** (e.g., Louisiana Iris, Siberian Iris) - Many irises thrive in wet soil but can also tolerate drier periods.
- **Bee Balm** (Monarda spp.) - This plant prefers moist soil but can adapt to drier conditions and attracts pollinators.
- **Elderberry** (Sambucus spp.) - A shrub that grows well in wet soil but can also tolerate dry spells once established.

Tips for Maximizing Rainwater Collection

With a few smart tips and tricks, you can maximize rainwater collection. Pay attention to your house, and you'll find plenty of structures that you can use to collect and store water. For example, gutters act as channels, directing water from your roof to your downspouts and collection systems. Keeping them clean is essential for efficient rainwater collection. When they're clogged with leaves, twigs, or debris, they can't effectively channel water, leading to overflow and waste. This can also damage your home's foundation. Regular cleaning ensures a smooth flow of rainwater, maximizing the amount you can collect.

Similarly, using dark-colored rain barrels is another simple way to improve rainwater harvesting. Algae thrive in sunlight. Clear or light-colored barrels allow sunlight to penetrate, promoting algae growth, which can clog spigots and make the water less suitable for irrigation.

Dark-colored barrels block sunlight, inhibiting algae growth, keeping your collected water clean and ready for use.

A first-flush diverter is another valuable addition to your system. The initial rainfall washes away accumulated dust, debris, and pollutants from your roof, resulting in dirty water. A first-flush diverter filters dirty water, redirecting it away from your collection system and ensuring that the water you collect is clean and safe for your garden.

Finally, consider the size of your roof, as it directly impacts the amount of rainwater you can collect. A larger roof surface area yields more water. Calculating the potential collection helps you determine the appropriate size and number of rain barrels or other collection systems you need. This calculation involves knowing your average rainfall and the square footage of your roof.

How do swales work?

For those with larger gardens, designing swales — shallow ditches that slow down, capture, and direct rainwater — can help distribute moisture evenly across the landscape, reducing the need for additional watering.

Swales are typically built along the contour of a slope, following the same elevation line. They slow down the water's flow, allowing it to spread out and soak into the soil, creating a temporary water reservoir. Rainwater flows down a slope, collecting in swales. Plants grow on the berm, the raised area on the side of the swale, benefit from the increased moisture. Swales are excellent for refilling underground water tables and reducing erosion.

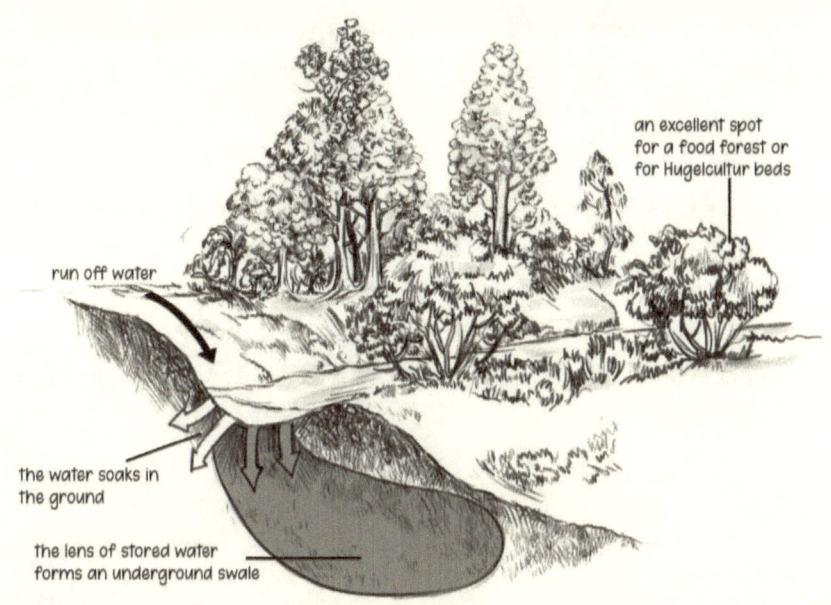

The benefits of swales are numerous. They improve soil moisture and plant growth, reduce runoff and erosion, replenish groundwater, and enhance biodiversity. Properly designed swales are essential to avoid waterlogging and erosion. The size and spacing of swales should be determined based on the landscape, soil type, and rainfall patterns. They work best on gentle slopes. Just make sure to check your local construction laws and regulations before building them.

Drought-Resistant Gardening

In regions prone to drought, selecting drought-resistant plants is crucial. These plants thrive in dry conditions, requiring less frequent irrigation. Succulents, lavender, and rosemary are excellent choices as they store water in their leaves or have deep root systems that tap into lower soil moisture levels. Implementing xeriscaping principles—landscaping with plants that naturally require less water—can transform your garden into a resilient, low-maintenance oasis.

Additional Water Conservation Tips

Here are some tips to increase water conservation on your landscape

- **Water Deeply and Less Frequently** - Encourage deep root growth by watering thoroughly but infrequently.
- **Water in the Morning or Evening** - Reduce evaporation by watering during the evening or night.
- **Use Greywater** - If possible, repurpose household greywater (from showers or laundry) for irrigation, ensuring it's free from harmful chemicals.
- **Monitor Soil Moisture** - Use a moisture meter or simply check the soil with your finger to determine when watering is necessary.
- **Mulch** - Apply a layer of mulch around your plants to retain moisture and reduce the need for frequent watering.

With your garden's water needs met sustainably, you're ready to tackle the challenge of limited space. In the following part, we'll uncover the secrets of maximizing small spaces with companion planting, including vertical gardens, raised beds, and more.

Maximizing Small Spaces with Companion Planting

Limited space shouldn't limit your gardening dreams. Whether you have a tiny balcony, a compact patio, or just a small patch of earth, you can still cultivate a thriving garden. The key is to think creatively and utilize every available bit of space. So, let's look at some clever ways to maximize small spaces, starting with a technique that takes your gardening to new heights: vertical gardening.

1. Vertical gardening

When working with limited space, every square inch of your garden counts, and companion planting can help make the most of it. Vertical gardening is an innovative approach that maximizes space by growing plants upward, making it ideal for small areas or urban settings. Think of it as creating a multi-story garden. Here are some practical examples:

Trellises and Arbors - Utilize trellises or arbors to support climbing plants like beans, peas, cucumbers, and flowering vines. This method not only saves ground space for low-growing plants like lettuce or radishes but also enhances air circulation, reducing the risk of diseases. Using trellises and arbors can also provide shade for heat-sensitive plants.

Living Walls - Install vertical structures on walls or fences and cover them with a variety of plants, including herbs, succulents, or ferns. Living walls can improve air quality, provide insulation, and add aesthetic appeal to indoor or outdoor spaces.

Vertical Planters - Use tiered planters, hanging pots, or stackable systems to grow herbs, strawberries, or leafy greens. These setups are perfect for balconies or patios, allowing easy access and efficient use of vertical space.

Pallet Gardens - Repurpose wooden pallets by filling them with soil and planting shallow-rooted vegetables or flowers. Lean the pallet against a wall or fence to create a rustic, space-saving garden.

Gutter Gardens - Mount cleaned and sealed rain gutters horizontally on a wall or fence, then fill them with soil to grow herbs, lettuce, or strawberries. This method is an excellent way to recycle materials and create additional planting space.

Container gardening

If you've got a tiny balcony, a sun-drenched patio, or simply crave the flexibility of a movable garden, then give container gardening a try. In just a few easy steps you can transform a barren outdoor area into a lush, vibrant haven.

Imagine transforming a cramped space into a miniature oasis where vibrant plants thrive in carefully selected pots, tubs, and other containers. This method provides an exceptional degree of control, allowing you to fine-tune the growing environment. By selecting the perfect potting mix, you can optimize soil quality for specific plant needs, ensuring excellent drainage and aeration, preventing root rot, and promoting robust growth. Furthermore, containers allow you to manipulate sunlight exposure with ease. Simply move them around to shield them from the intense heat or provide more access to sunlight.

You can manipulate the gardening setup while companion planting to enhance growth. For example, strawberry and borage can thrive in a large container placed in a sunny spot. Herbs and flowers, with their compact growth habits, are particularly well-suited for growing

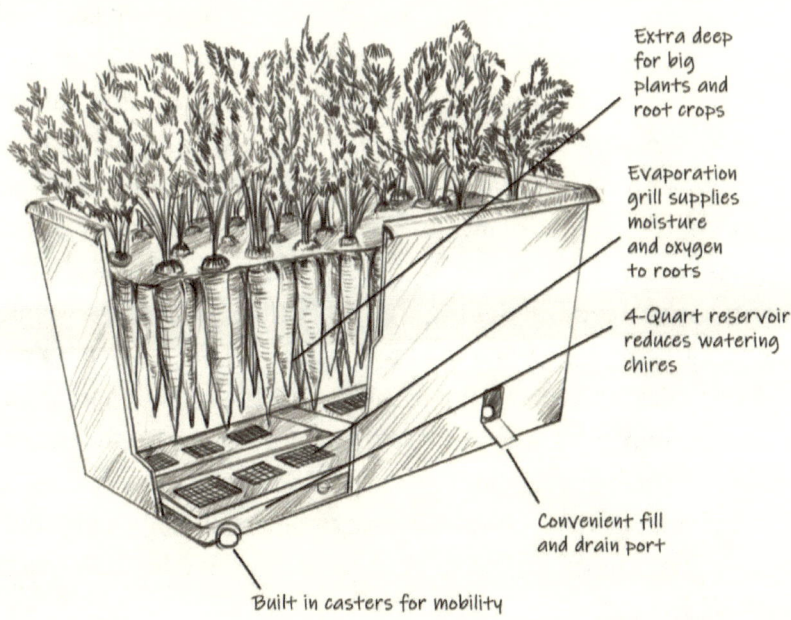

Extra deep for big plants and root crops

Evaporation grill supplies moisture and oxygen to roots

4-Quart reservoir reduces watering chires

Convenient fill and drain port

Built in casters for mobility

together in containers. Similarly, many vegetables and even dwarf fruit trees can thrive in containers.

Container gardening is like giving your plants a little mobile home. You can easily move them around, taking care of their many requirements through different seasons. Plus, containers offer a wide range of aesthetic and functional choices, from elegant ceramic pots that add a touch of sophistication to your patio to practical plastic tubs that maximize space and drainage. Just remember to ensure adequate drainage holes at the bottom to prevent waterlogging, a common pitfall in container gardening.

Now, let's explore the art of plant partnerships within the confines of a container. Coriander, thyme, and parsley are excellent choices for container cultivation, thriving in the confined space while providing a constant supply of fresh flavors. Cherry tomatoes when paired with marigolds create a visually appealing and mutually beneficial combination. These compact arrangements allow you to cultivate a diverse array of plants without requiring extensive land, maximizing productivity in even the smallest spaces.

A high-quality potting mix is essential for a flourishing container garden. A good potting mix ensures optimal aeration and water retention. You can also consider incorporating slow-release fertilizers into the mix to ensure your plants receive a consistent and balanced supply of nutrients throughout their growth cycle. Regular watering and occasional pruning are also crucial for maintaining the health and vigor of your container plants. If you want to delve deeper into the intricacies of container gardening, check out my book, "**Beginner's Guide to Container Gardening**." It provides a comprehensive guide to planning, preparing, and planting your own container garden, covering topics such as suitable plant selection, soil preparation, watering techniques, pest control, and general care. Flip the pages to the fourth chapter in Beginner's Guide to Container Gardening, and you'll find a long list of container-ready plant mix recipes tailored to different plant types to give your container garden the perfect foundation for success.

Raised beds

Raised beds are a simple yet powerful and practical way to take control of your growing space, especially if you're dealing with poor soil, tricky weather, or just want a more comfortable gardening experience. They offer a wide range of benefits including:

- **Soil Control** - Tired of battling heavy clay or nutrient-poor soil? Raised beds let you create the perfect growing medium. By adding ingredients like compost, peat moss, or perlite, you can customize the soil to fit your plants' needs perfectly. This way, they get the right nutrition and grow strong, so you get healthier and bigger plants.
- **Drainage Dynamo** - Say goodbye to waterlogged roots! Raised beds provide excellent drainage, ensuring that air reaches the roots, which prevents rot and encourages healthy growth. This is especially helpful in areas with heavy rainfall or clay soil.
- **Back-Friendly Gardening** - No more bending or stooping! The elevated height of raised beds makes planting, weeding, and harvesting a breeze, especially for those with limited mobility, chronic back pain, or those who simply prefer a more ergonomic gardening experience.
- **Pest Prevention** - Raised beds function as a physical barrier, deterring ground-dwelling pests like slugs, snails, and voles. The elevated structure also minimizes soil compaction, which can harbor pests and diseases. Additionally, you can easily install protective coverings, such as netting or row covers, to shield plants from airborne pests, birds, and harsh weather conditions.
- **Extended Growing Season** - Raised beds warm up faster in the spring, allowing you to start planting earlier. You can also easily add cold frames or hoop houses to extend your growing season into the late fall or even winter months.
- **Allelopathy Management** - Separate plants that don't play well together! Raised beds provide a clear physical separation,

preventing chemical interactions and allowing for the cultivation of incompatible species in close proximity.
- **Kid-Friendly Gardening** - Create a dedicated raised bed for your children to foster a sense of ownership and encourage hands-on learning about plant growth, enabling them to actively participate in planting, weeding, and harvesting! They'll love having their own space to plant and grow their favorite vegetables and flowers. Imagine the joy of eating their own homegrown peas or sun-ripened tomatoes!
- **Efficient Watering** - The defined boundaries of the beds prevent water runoff, ensuring that moisture is delivered directly to the root zone. Raised beds make it easier to water your plants precisely, reducing water waste and ensuring your plants receive the moisture they need.

Building Your Raised Bed Oasis: Tips & Tricks

Let's get down to the basics. Here's everything you need to know to construct your very own raised bed garden:

- **Size it Right** - Aim for a height of 12-24 inches / 30-60 cm for ample root growth and comfortable access. Keep the width manageable (no more than 4 feet / 120 cm) so you can reach the center without stepping on the soil, preventing compaction. Length can be adjusted to fit your garden space and needs.
- **Soil Perfection** - Use a high-quality soil mix. A blend of topsoil, compost, and peat moss or coconut coir is a good starting point. Add perlite or vermiculite for improved drainage, especially in clay-heavy areas. Incorporate slow-release fertilizers for sustained nutrient availability.
- **Location, Location, Location** - Choose a sunny spot with good drainage, receiving at least 6-8 hours of direct sunlight per day for most vegetables. Consider the mature size of your plants and ensure adequate spacing to prevent overcrowding. Orient the beds to maximize sunlight exposure, particularly if you live in a cooler climate or during the winter season.

- **Level Up** - Ensure your raised bed is level to prevent uneven watering and soil erosion. Use a leveling tool and even out the soil surface.

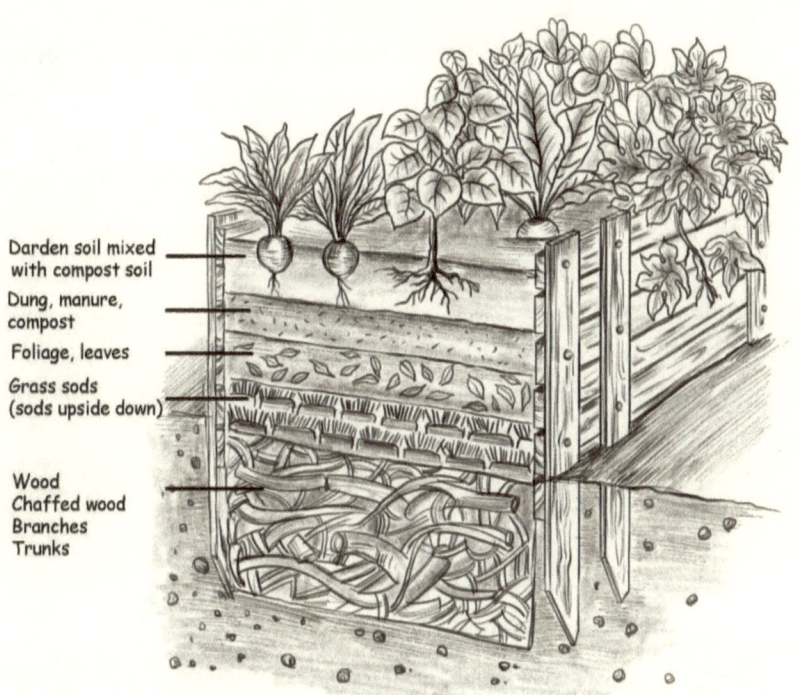

Raised bad filling in layers

Companion planting within these beds can yield impressive results. Managing soil compaction is essential, so avoid walking on the soil and regularly aerate it to keep it loose and friable. Raised beds encourage a dynamic planting approach where you can easily rotate crops and introduce new pairings each season, maintaining soil vitality and reducing pest cycles.

Building raised beds is often a straightforward project, using materials that are both durable and environmentally friendly. Wood is a popular choice due to its natural aesthetic and availability, but you can also look into using recycled materials like old bricks or cinder blocks. When constructing your raised bed, aim for an optimal height of 12 to 24 inches (30-60 cm). This allows ample room for root growth and ensures easy access. Keep the width manageable, typically no wider than four feet (120 cm), so you can reach the center from either side without stepping into the bed. This setup not only preserves soil structure by preventing compaction but maximizes your planting area. As you fill your raised bed, use a mix of high-quality soil and organic matter to create a fertile environment for your plants, enhancing both health and productivity.

Raised beds offer myriad benefits, helping you overcome a number of challenges, such as poor soil quality or limited space. They provide superior drainage, which is crucial for preventing waterlogged roots that can lead to plant diseases. Some soils, such as heavy clay soils, become compacted quickly. Raised beds can prevent this from happening by allowing better air circulation. Moreover, the elevated design makes them more accessible for planting, weeding, and harvesting without the need to bend or stoop. This ease of access is particularly advantageous for those with mobility issues or anyone who prefers a more comfortable gardening experience.

For an in-depth guide to raised bed gardening, including detailed instructions on building, planting, and maintaining your raised bed, check out my book, **"The Complete Guide to Raised Bed Gardening."** It's your one-stop resource for everything you need to know about raised beds.

Maximizing Yields with Succession Planting

A practical tip for small-space gardening is to incorporate succession planting. It involves planting crops in stages so you can enjoy an uninterrupted harvest all year long. Instead of planting everything at once, you spread out your planting over weeks or even months, ensuring a continuous supply of fresh produce.

This method is especially effective for fast-growing crops or those with varying maturity times. Leafy greens like lettuce and spinach are perfect candidates. You can plant a new batch every couple of weeks, replacing harvested plants with fresh seedlings. Root vegetables, such as radishes, are also ideal. Their quick growth allows you to plant multiple rounds in the same space, keeping your garden productive and your harvest manageable.

A planting calendar is essential for successful succession planting. Begin by marking your last spring frost and first fall frost to identify your growing season. Start planting cool-weather crops like lettuce and radishes in early spring and continue planting them every few weeks. As summer arrives, switch to heat-loving plants like beans or summer squash. When fall approaches, return to cool-weather crops to keep your garden going until frost. This careful timing makes the most of your growing season.

Succession planting also helps control pests. Planting a different crop every few weeks makes it hard for pests to settle in. This disrupts their life cycles, reducing infestations and the need for chemicals. Plus, keeping your soil covered with plants prevents erosion, maintains fertility, and suppresses weeds, saving you time and effort.

There's a lot of room for you to experiment with different planting combinations and try out different schedules to find what works best. Maybe you'll find that radishes and mustard greens are your favorite pairing or that growing carrots followed by beets gives you the best root vegetable harvest.

Maximizing Crop Yields Through Succession Planting

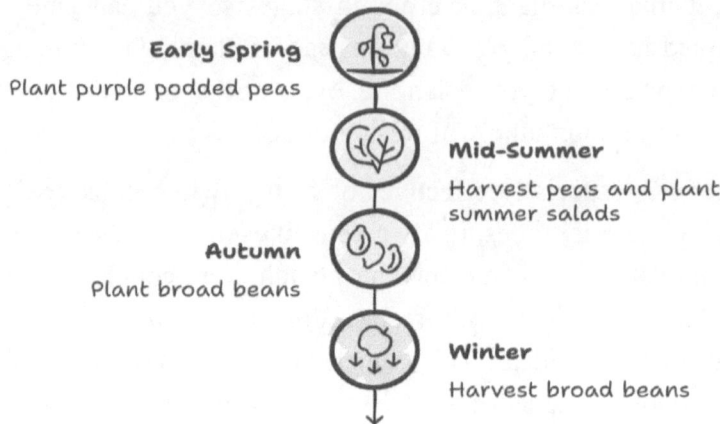

Each season is a chance to learn and improve, creating a vibrant and productive garden that feeds you throughout the year. Here are some practical examples you can try:

1. **Staggered Planting of the Same Crop** - Planting the same vegetable at intervals ensures a steady supply. For instance, sowing lettuce seeds every two weeks allows for continuous harvesting as each batch matures at different times.
2. **Sequential Planting with Different Crops** - After harvesting an early-maturing crop, plant a different crop in the same place. For example, after harvesting early peas, you can plant tomatoes, peppers, or eggplants in the same area.
3. **Planting Varieties with Different Maturity Dates** - Choose varieties of the same vegetable that mature at different times. For example, planting both early and late-maturing varieties of sweet corn ensures a prolonged harvest period.
4. **Intercropping Fast and Slow-Growing Crops** - Plant quick-maturing crops alongside slower-growing ones. Radishes, which mature rapidly, can be planted between

rows of carrots. The radishes will be harvested before the carrots need more space.

5. **Relay Planting** - Start a new crop in the same space before the previous one finishes. For instance, sowing bush beans between rows of maturing spinach allows the beans to establish as the spinach is harvested.

Your Own Planting Calendar

Download my seed starting and planting chart from www.sophiemckay.com to make the process of planning your garden completely hassle-free.

The charts will help you decide which plants you should grow during different seasons so you get an abundant harvest and make the most of your garden.

Intercropping Fast and Slow-Growing Crops

Intercropping is a clever gardening technique that goes beyond simply planting crops side by side. It involves strategically pairing plants that benefit each other to reap maximum benefits. This method is especially valuable for maximizing space and enhancing overall garden health.

One of the key benefits of intercropping is efficient space utilization. By combining plants with different growth habits and needs, you can make the most of every corner of your garden.

For example, plant lettuce beneath taller crops like tomatoes or peppers. The taller plants will provide shade to the heat-sensitive lettuce, keeping it cool and preventing bolting (going to seed prematurely). This mutually beneficial relationship allows both plants to thrive.

Intercropping also helps deter pests. The diverse mix of plant species prevents a single type of pest from thriving, which is usually the case in monocultures (single-crop plantings). The variety of scents and textures confuses pests, making it harder for them to locate their preferred host plants. For example, aromatic herbs like basil or marigolds planted among your vegetables can ward off many common garden pests.

In addition to the above, the technique works wonders for soil health. Different plants have varying root systems, which can improve soil structure and enhance nutrient availability. Deep-rooted plants break up compacted soil, drawing up nutrients from lower layers, while shallow-rooted plants utilize surface nutrients. The diverse root networks create a more balanced and fertile soil environment.

Here are some tips to include intercropping in your companion planting setup are:

- **Consider Plant Compatibility** - Research which plants grow well together. Pay attention to their sunlight, water, and nutrient requirements. Some plants may compete for resources or have allelopathic effects (releasing chemicals that inhibit the growth of other plants).
- **Staggered Planting Rows** - Alternate different crops in staggered rows to ensure each has enough space and light. For example, a row of root vegetables like carrots might be interspersed with a row of leafy greens like spinach or lettuce.
- **Layered Planting** - Combine deep-rooted plants with shallow-rooted plants to optimize soil use and prevent nutrient competition. For instance, plant carrots (deep-rooted) alongside lettuce (shallow-rooted).
- **Succession Planting within Intercropping** - Combine intercropping with succession planting for continuous

harvests. As one intercropped crop is harvested, replace it with another compatible crop.
- **Utilize Vertical Space** - Use trellises or other vertical frameworks to grow vining plants like beans or cucumbers alongside shorter crops. This maximizes vertical space and provides shade for shade-loving plants.
- **Observe and Adjust** - Pay close attention to how your intercropped plants are growing and interacting. Be prepared to adjust your planting plan as needed.

Water, soil, and space make up the foundation of a flourishing garden. We explored the different ways we can manipulate these variables to our advantage. A healthy, thriving garden requires careful observation and problem-solving. With the methods above you can ensure that your plants get the care they need regardless of where you live, the type of soil you have to work with, or scarce water supply.

Now that we know how to stretch our resources and manipulate our environment to our advantage, it's time to grab our shovels and start planting. Up next, we'll look at common plant pairings and cheat sheets for finding the best combinations.

CHAPTER 4

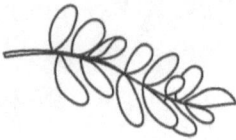

Companion Pairings & Cheat Sheets

Imagine walking through your garden and seeing a vibrant ecosystem where every plant has a specific role, working together in harmony. As a gardener, your goal is to understand the unique characteristics of each plant. This allows you to match them in ways that enhance their growth, deter pests, and improve yields. Let's explore how to harness your plants' unique abilities to create a thriving and resilient garden.

Each plant in your garden has distinct needs and characteristics that, when understood, can guide you in creating successful pairings. Nutrient requirements play a crucial role; some plants, like leafy greens, are heavy feeders, requiring rich, nitrogen-filled soil, while others, such as root vegetables, may thrive in less fertile conditions. Growth patterns also vary; some plants grow tall and sprawling, providing support or shade to other plant varieties, while others remain compact and low to the ground. Respecting these needs is the first step in crafting a garden where plants coexist and support each other.

Matching plants based on compatibility involves considering light and water needs as well as root depth. Some plants relish full sun, basking in its warmth, while others prefer the cool refuge of partial shade. Similarly, water needs can vary widely, with certain plants thriving in moist conditions and others requiring well-drained soil. Root depth is another essential factor; pairing deep-rooted plants with shallow-rooted ones can prevent competition for nutrients and increase available space.

The Dynamics of a Self-sustaining and Regenerative Ecosystem in the Garden

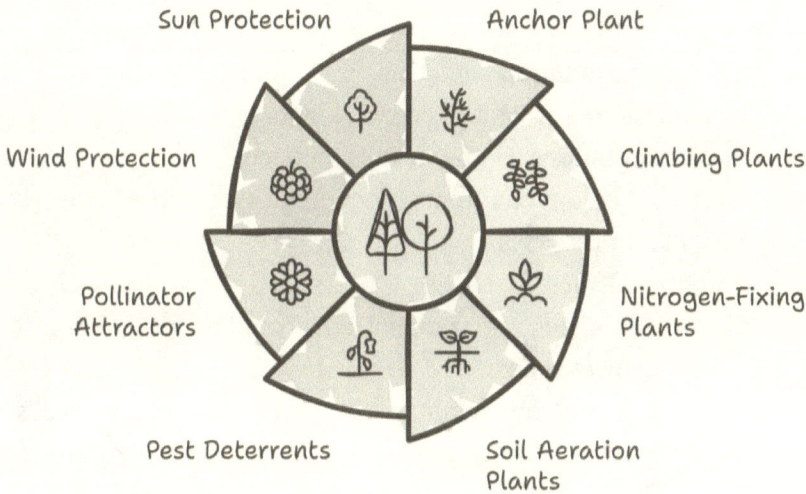

In the following sections, we will explore some of the most popular vegetables, followed by a look at common fruits, herbs, and flowers that thrive in various gardens. After covering these essentials, we'll move onto beginner-friendly plant mixes that offer an easy starting point for new gardeners. We will also dive into the Three Sisters pairing, a classic companion planting technique that has been used for centuries. Additionally, we will discuss the benefits of combining perennial and annual plants, ensuring a balanced and sustainable garden throughout the seasons.

Vegetable Companion Planting Guide

Bright, colorful vegetables are a dinner table staple. In this section, we'll look at different vegetables and their best or worst companion. You'll find a simplified version of the lists below at the back of the book for quick reference if you want to double-check anything while planting. For now, let's delve into the world of planting mysteries, explore enduring friendships and enmities between different plants.

Asparagus

- **Good Companions**: Tomatoes.
  Tomatoes repel asparagus beetles.
- **Bad Companions**: Garlic, onions, potatoes.
  Garlic and onions can stunt asparagus growth, and potatoes compete for nutrients.
- Additional Notes:
    - Asparagus is a perennial and should be planted in a dedicated bed.
    - Use **mulch** to retain soil moisture and suppress weeds.
    - Harvest asparagus spears when they are 6–8 inches (15–20 cm) tall and before the tips begin to open.

Beans (Bush)

- **Good Companions**: Carrots, cucumbers, corn, celery, potatoes.
  Beans fix nitrogen in the soil, benefiting heavy feeders like corn and potatoes. Carrots and cucumbers benefit from the nitrogen-rich soil.
- **Bad Companions**: Garlic, onions, shallots.
  Alliums can inhibit the growth of beans by releasing chemicals that stunt their development.
- Additional Notes:
    - Beans are excellent for **crop rotation** as they enrich the soil with nitrogen.
    - Avoid planting beans in the same spot year after year to prevent disease buildup.
    - Use **row covers** to protect against bean beetles.

Beans (Pole)

- **Good Companions**: Corn, radishes, spinach.
  Corn provides a natural trellis for pole beans, and radishes deter pests. Spinach provides ground cover, retaining soil moisture.
- **Bad Companions**: Beets, garlic, onions, shallots.
  Similar to bush beans, pole beans are inhibited by alliums. Beets compete for space and nutrients.
- **Additional Notes**:
  - Pole beans benefit from **marigolds** and **nasturtiums**, which repel pests.
  - Provide sturdy support for pole beans to prevent them from collapsing under their own weight.
  - Harvest beans regularly to encourage continuous production.

Beets

- **Good Companions**: Broccoli, Brussels sprouts, cabbage, cauliflower, lettuce, onions.
  Beets grow well with brassicas and benefit from the pest-repellent properties of onions.
- **Bad Companions**: Pole beans.
  Pole beans can stunt beet growth.
- **Additional Notes**:
  - Beets prefer cool weather and should be planted early in the spring or late in the fall.
  - Thin beet seedlings early to prevent overcrowding and improve root development.
  - Harvest beets when they are young and tender for the best flavor.

Broccoli

- **Good Companions**: Beets, celery, onions, potatoes.
  Onions repel pests like aphids, and celery provides ground cover to retain moisture. Potatoes benefit from the nitrogen-fixing abilities of broccoli.

- **Bad Companions**: Strawberries, tomatoes, pole beans. Strawberries and tomatoes compete for nutrients, and pole beans can stunt broccoli growth.
- **Additional Notes**:
    - Broccoli is a heavy feeder and benefits from **compost** or well-rotted manure.
    - Use **row covers** to protect against cabbage worms and aphids.
    - Harvest the main head before it flowers, and side shoots will continue to produce.

Brussels Sprouts

- **Good Companions**: Beets, celery, onions, potatoes. Brussels sprouts benefit from the pest-repellent properties of onions and the nitrogen-fixing abilities of beans.
- **Bad Companions**: Strawberries, tomatoes. Strawberries and tomatoes compete for nutrients.
- **Additional Notes**:
    - Brussels sprouts are heavy feeders and benefit from **compost** or well-rotted manure.
    - Use **row covers** to protect against pests like cabbage worms.
    - Harvest Brussels sprouts when the sprouts are firm and about 1–2 inches (2.5–5 cm) in diameter.

Cabbage

- **Good Companions**: Beets, celery, onions, potatoes. Onions repel pests, and celery provides ground cover. Potatoes benefit from the nitrogen-fixing abilities of cabbage.
- **Bad Companions**: Strawberries, tomatoes, pole beans. Strawberries and tomatoes compete for nutrients, and pole beans can stunt cabbage growth.
- **Additional Notes**:
    - Cabbage is susceptible to pests like cabbage worms and aphids. Use **row covers** or plant **nasturtiums** nearby to deter pests.

- Rotate cabbage annually to prevent soil-borne diseases like clubroot.
- Harvest cabbage heads when they are firm and dense.

Carrots

- **Good Companions**: Beans, leeks, lettuce, onions, peas, tomatoes.
  Onions and leeks repel carrot flies, while beans and peas fix nitrogen in the soil, benefiting carrots. Lettuce provides shade, keeping the soil cool.
- **Bad Companions**: Dill, parsnips, potatoes.
  Dill can attract pests harmful to carrots, and parsnips compete for space and nutrients. Potatoes can stunt carrot growth due to their aggressive root systems.
- **Additional Notes**:
  - Carrots thrive in loose, sandy soil. Avoid heavy clay soils, which can cause misshapen roots.
  - Thin carrot seedlings early to prevent overcrowding.
  - Use **row covers** to protect against carrot flies.

Cauliflower

- **Good Companions**: Beets, celery, onions, potatoes.
  Similar to broccoli and cabbage, cauliflower benefits from onions and celery. Potatoes benefit from the nitrogen-fixing abilities of cauliflower.
- **Bad Companions**: Strawberries, tomatoes, pole beans.
  Avoid planting near strawberries or tomatoes to prevent competition.
- **Additional Notes**:
  - Cauliflower is sensitive to temperature fluctuations. Plant in cool weather and provide consistent moisture.
  - Use **row covers** to protect against pests like cabbage worms.
  - Blanch the heads by tying the outer leaves over the heads to protect them from sunlight.

Celery

- **Good Companions**: Beans, cabbage, cauliflower, leeks, onions, tomatoes.
  Celery benefits from the shade of taller plants and the pest-repellent properties of onions.
- **Bad Companions**: Corn, potatoes.
  Corn and potatoes compete for nutrients and space.
- **Additional Notes**:
  - Celery is a moisture-loving plant and benefits from consistent watering.
  - Use **mulch** to retain soil moisture and suppress weeds.
  - Harvest celery stalks when they are firm and crisp.

Corn

- **Good Companions**: Beans, cucumbers, peas, potatoes, pumpkins, squash.
  Corn provides support for climbing plants like beans and cucumbers.
- **Bad Companions**: Tomatoes.
  Tomatoes and corn attract the same pests, such as corn earworms.
- **Additional Notes**:
  - Corn is wind-pollinated, so plant in blocks rather than rows for better pollination.
  - Use **mulch** to retain soil moisture and suppress weeds.
  - Harvest corn when the silks turn brown and the kernels are plump.

Cucumbers

- **Good Companions**: Beans, corn, peas, radishes.
  Corn provides a natural trellis for cucumbers to climb, and radishes deter cucumber beetles. Beans fix nitrogen in the soil, benefiting cucumbers.
- **Bad Companions**: Potatoes.
  Potatoes and cucumbers compete for nutrients and water, and both are susceptible to similar pests.
- **Additional Notes**:

- Cucumbers benefit from **nasturtiums** and **marigolds**, which repel aphids and beetles.
- Provide consistent moisture to prevent bitter fruit.
- Train cucumbers vertically to save space and improve air circulation.

Eggplant

- **Good Companions**: Beans, spinach.
  Beans fix nitrogen in the soil, benefiting eggplants.
- **Bad Companions**: None significant.
  Eggplants are relatively easygoing but prefer not to compete with heavy feeders.
- **Additional Notes**:
  - Eggplants benefit from **marigolds** and **basil**, which repel pests.
  - Provide consistent moisture to prevent blossom-end rot.
  - Harvest eggplants when the skin is glossy and firm.

Garlic

- **Good Companions**: Beets, carrots, cucumbers, lettuce, tomatoes.
  Garlic repels pests like aphids and spider mites.
- **Bad Companions**: Beans, peas, asparagus.
  Garlic can inhibit the growth of legumes and asparagus.
- **Additional Notes**:
  - Garlic is a natural pest deterrent and can be planted throughout the garden.
  - Plant garlic in the fall for a summer harvest.
  - Harvest garlic when the lower leaves turn brown and dry.

Kale

- **Good Companions**: Beets, celery, cucumbers, onions, spinach.
  Kale grows well with nitrogen-fixing plants and benefits from the pest-repellent properties of onions.

- **Bad Companions**: Strawberries, tomatoes.
  Strawberries and tomatoes compete for nutrients.
- **Additional Notes**:
  - Kale is a hardy plant and can tolerate cooler temperatures.
  - Use **row covers** to protect against pests like cabbage worms.
  - Harvest kale leaves when they are young and tender for the best flavor.

Leeks

- **Good Companions**: Carrots, celery, onions, strawberries.
  Leeks repel carrot flies and benefit from the shade of taller plants.
- **Bad Companions**: Beans, peas.
  Leeks can inhibit the growth of legumes.
- **Additional Notes**:
  - Leeks prefer well-drained soil and full sun.
  - Use **mulch** to retain soil moisture and suppress weeds.
  - Harvest leeks when the stems are about 1 inch (2.5cm) in diameter.

Lettuce

- **Good Companions**: Beets, carrots, cucumbers, onions, radishes, strawberries, tomatoes.
  Lettuce benefits from the shade of taller plants like tomatoes and the pest-repellent properties of onions. Radishes deter pests like aphids.
- **Bad Companions**: Cabbage, celery.
  Cabbage and lettuce compete for nutrients, and celery can attract pests harmful to lettuce.
- **Additional Notes**:
  - Lettuce prefers cool weather and can bolt (go to seed) in hot temperatures. Plant in partial shade during the summer.

- Use **row covers** to protect against pests like slugs and aphids.
- Harvest outer leaves regularly to encourage continuous growth.

Okra

- **Good Companions**: Beans, cucumbers, peppers.
  Beans fix nitrogen in the soil, benefiting okra.
- **Bad Companions**: None significant.
  Okra is relatively easygoing but prefers not to compete with heavy feeders.
- **Additional Notes**:
  - Okra thrives in hot weather and well-drained soil.
  - Use **mulch** to retain soil moisture and suppress weeds.
  - Harvest okra pods when they are 2–4 inches (5–10 cm) long for the best flavor.

Onions

- **Good Companions**: Beets, carrots, lettuce, tomatoes.
  Onions repel pests like carrot flies and aphids.
- **Bad Companions**: Beans, peas, asparagus.
  Onions can stunt the growth of legumes and asparagus.
- **Additional Notes**:
  - Onions are heavy feeders and benefit from **compost** or well-rotted manure.
  - Use **mulch** to retain soil moisture and suppress weeds.
  - Harvest onions when the tops fall over and begin to dry.

Parsnips

- **Good Companions**: Beans, carrots, onions, peas.
  Parsnips grow well with nitrogen-fixing plants like beans and peas.
- **Bad Companions**: None significant.
  Parsnips are relatively easygoing but prefer not to compete with heavy feeders.
- **Additional Notes**:

- Parsnips prefer deep, loose soil for optimal root growth.
- Thin parsnip seedlings early to prevent overcrowding.
- Harvest parsnips after the first frost for the best flavor.

Peas

- **Good Companions**: Carrots, corn, cucumbers, radishes, turnips, beans.
  Peas fix nitrogen in the soil, benefiting nearby plants. Radishes deter pests like aphids.
- **Bad Companions**: Garlic, onions, shallots, potatoes.
  Alliums stunt pea growth, and potatoes compete for nutrients and space.
- **Additional Notes**:
  - Peas are cool-season crops and should be planted early in the spring or late in the fall.
  - Provide support for climbing varieties to improve air circulation and reduce disease risk.
  - Rotate peas annually to prevent soil-borne diseases.

Peppers

- **Good Companions**: Carrots, onions, spinach, tomatoes.
  Onions help deter pests like aphids, and spinach provides ground cover to retain soil moisture. Tomatoes and peppers share similar growing conditions and can thrive together.
- **Bad Companions**: Beans, brassicas.
  Beans can stunt the growth of peppers, and brassicas compete for nutrients.
- **Additional Notes**:
  - Peppers benefit from **basil** and **oregano**, which improve flavor and repel pests.
  - Avoid overwatering, as peppers prefer well-drained soil.
  - Mulch around peppers to retain moisture and suppress weeds.

Potatoes

- **Good Companions**: Beans, corn, cabbage, eggplant, peas.
  Beans and peas fix nitrogen in the soil, benefiting potatoes.

- **Bad Companions**: Cucumbers, pumpkins, squash, tomatoes.
  These plants compete for nutrients and are susceptible to similar diseases.
- **Additional Notes**:
  - Potatoes are heavy feeders and benefit from **compost** or well-rotted manure.
  - Hill soil around potato plants to protect tubers from sunlight and prevent greening.
  - Rotate potatoes annually to prevent soil-borne diseases like blight.

Pumpkins

- **Good Companions**: Corn, beans.
  Corn provides shade, and beans fix nitrogen in the soil.
- **Bad Companions**: Potatoes.
  Potatoes and pumpkins compete for nutrients and space.
- **Additional Notes**:
  - Pumpkins are heavy feeders and benefit from **compost** or well-rotted manure.
  - Use **mulch** to retain soil moisture and suppress weeds.
  - Harvest pumpkins when the rind is hard and the stem begins to dry.

Radishes

- **Good Companions**: Beans, carrots, cucumbers, lettuce, peas, spinach.
  Radishes deter pests like cucumber beetles and grow quickly, making them great fillers.
- **Bad Companions**: Cabbage, cauliflower, broccoli.
  Radishes can attract pests harmful to brassicas.
- **Additional Notes**:
  - Radishes are fast-growing and can be used as a **trap crop** for pests.
  - Thin radishes early to prevent overcrowding and improve root development.

- Harvest radishes when they are young and tender for the best flavor.

Rutabagas

- **Good Companions**: Peas, beans.
  Rutabagas grow well with nitrogen-fixing plants.
- **Bad Companions**: Potatoes.
  Potatoes and rutabagas compete for nutrients.
- **Additional Notes**:
  - Rutabagas prefer cool weather and consistent moisture.
  - Thin rutabaga seedlings early to prevent overcrowding.
  - Harvest rutabagas when they are 3–5 inches (7.5–12.5 cm) in diameter.

Spinach

- **Good Companions**: Cabbage, cauliflower, celery, eggplant, onions, peas.
  Spinach grows well with nitrogen-fixing plants like peas and benefits from the shade of taller plants. Onions repel pests like aphids.
- **Bad Companions**: Potatoes.
  Potatoes can overshadow spinach and compete for nutrients.
- **Additional Notes**:
  - Spinach is a cool-season crop and should be planted early in the spring or late in the fall.
  - Use **mulch** to retain soil moisture and suppress weeds.
  - Harvest spinach leaves when they are young and tender for the best flavor.

Sweet Potatoes

- **Good Companions**: Beans.
  Beans fix nitrogen in the soil, benefiting sweet potatoes.
- **Bad Companions**: None significant.
  Sweet potatoes are relatively easygoing but prefer not to compete with heavy feeders.

- **Additional Notes**:
    - Sweet potatoes require warm soil and plenty of space to spread.
    - Use **mulch** to retain soil moisture and suppress weeds.
    - Harvest sweet potatoes when the leaves begin to yellow and die back.

Tomatoes

- **Good Companions**: Carrots, celery, onions, lettuce, spinach.
  Carrots and tomatoes can share space well, as carrots loosen the soil for tomato roots. Onions and celery repel pests like aphids and spider mites. Lettuce and spinach provide ground cover, retaining soil moisture.
- **Bad Companions**: Brassicas (e.g., broccoli, cabbage), corn, potatoes.
  Brassicas and tomatoes compete for nutrients, and planting near corn can attract the same pests. Potatoes and tomatoes are both susceptible to blight, so planting them together increases the risk of disease spread.
- **Additional Notes**:
    - Tomatoes benefit from **marigolds** and **basil**, which deter pests like nematodes and whiteflies.
    - Avoid planting near **walnut trees**, as they release juglone, a chemical that inhibits tomato growth.
    - Rotate tomatoes annually to prevent soil-borne diseases like fusarium wilt.

Turnips

- **Good Companions**: Peas, beans.
  Turnips grow well with nitrogen-fixing plants.
- **Bad Companions**: Potatoes.
  Potatoes and turnips compete for nutrients.
- **Additional Notes**:
    - Turnips are fast-growing and can be used as a **cover crop**.
    - Thin turnip seedlings early to prevent overcrowding.

- Harvest turnips when they are young and tender for the best flavor.

Zucchini/Squash

- **Good Companions**: Beans, corn, radishes.
  Corn provides shade, and beans fix nitrogen in the soil.
- **Bad Companions**: Potatoes.
  Potatoes and squash compete for nutrients and space.
- **Additional Notes**:
    - Squash plants are susceptible to pests like squash bugs and vine borers. Use **row covers** or plant **nasturtiums** nearby to deter pests.
    - Provide consistent moisture to prevent blossom-end rot.
    - Harvest squash when the skin is tender and the fruit is small for the best flavor.
    - Train squash vines to grow vertically to save space and improve air circulation.
    - Avoid planting near potatoes, as they compete for nutrients and can attract similar pests.

Companion Planting Guide for Fruits

Now that we've covered the best and worst vegetable combinations, let's turn our attention to our fruit trees and bushes. Let's learn which plants go well with them and which to avoid.

Apple

- **Good Companions**: Chives, garlic, clover, dill, yarrow, nasturtiums, comfrey, borage, chamomile, mint, tansy, lavender, rosemary, thyme, sage, marigolds, carrots, beets, spinach, peas, beans, lettuce.
  These plants deter pests like aphids and attract beneficial insects like bees and hoverflies.
- **Bad Companions**: Potatoes, tomatoes, cabbage family, fennel, black walnut.
  Potatoes and tomatoes can spread diseases like blight, and cabbage-family plants compete for nutrients. Fennel and black walnuts release chemicals that inhibit apple tree growth.
- **Additional Notes**:
  - Plant **marigolds** and **nasturtiums** around apple trees to deter pests.
  - Avoid planting near **walnut trees**, as they release juglone, which is toxic to apples.
  - Prune apple trees regularly to improve air circulation and reduce disease risk.

Apricot

- **Good Companions**: Chives, garlic, clover, dill, yarrow, nasturtiums, comfrey, borage, chamomile, mint, tansy, lavender, rosemary, thyme, sage, marigolds, carrots, beets, spinach, peas, beans, lettuce.
  These plants deter pests like aphids and attract beneficial insects.
- **Bad Companions**: Potatoes, tomatoes, cabbage family, fennel, black walnut.
  Potatoes and tomatoes can spread diseases, and cabbage-family

plants compete for nutrients. Fennel and black walnut inhibit apricot growth.
- **Additional Notes**:
  - Plant **marigolds** and **nasturtiums** around apricot trees to deter pests.
  - Avoid planting near **walnut trees**, as they release juglone.
  - Prune apricot trees regularly to improve air circulation.

Blackcurrant

- **Good Companions**: Garlic, chives, marigolds, nasturtiums, chamomile, borage, comfrey, lavender, rosemary, thyme, sage, carrots, beets, spinach, lettuce, peas, beans.
  These plants deter pests like aphids and attract beneficial insects.
- **Bad Companions**: Fennel, black walnut, cabbage family. Fennel and black walnut inhibit blackcurrant growth, and cabbage-family plants compete for nutrients.
- **Additional Notes**:
  - Plant **marigolds** and **nasturtiums** around blackcurrant bushes to deter pests.
  - Avoid planting near **walnut trees**, as they release juglone.
  - Prune blackcurrant bushes regularly to improve air circulation.

Blueberry

- **Good Companions**: Phacelia, buckwheat, clover, lupine, azaleas, rhododendrons, pine trees, oak trees, strawberries, cranberries, huckleberries, legumes (beans, peas), mustard greens, radishes, carrots, beets, lettuce, spinach, dill, chamomile, yarrow, mint.
  These plants thrive in acidic soil and attract beneficial insects.
- **Bad Companions**: Cabbage family, tomatoes, potatoes, peppers, eggplant, cucumbers, melons.

Cabbage-family plants compete for nutrients, and nightshades can spread diseases.
- **Additional Notes**:
    - Blueberries prefer acidic soil (pH 4.5–5.5). Use pine needles or oak leaves as mulch to maintain acidity.
    - Plant **clover** or **lupine** nearby to fix nitrogen in the soil.
    - Avoid planting near **walnut trees**, as they release juglone.

Boysenberry

- **Good Companions**: Marigolds, nasturtiums, garlic, chives, dill, chamomile, thyme, borage, lavender, parsley, rosemary, sage, mint, tansy, comfrey, clover, yarrow, potatoes, asparagus, rhubarb, lettuce, spinach, carrots, beets, peas, beans.
These plants deter pests and attract beneficial insects.
- **Bad Companions**: Potatoes, tomatoes, peppers, eggplant, cucumbers, melons, squash, fennel, black walnut, cabbage family.
Nightshades can spread diseases, and cabbage-family plants compete for nutrients.
- **Additional Notes**:
    - Plant **marigolds** and **nasturtiums** around boysenberry bushes to deter pests.
    - Avoid planting near **walnut trees**, as they release juglone.
    - Prune boysenberry bushes regularly to improve air circulation.

Cherry

- **Good Companions**: Chives, garlic, clover, dill, yarrow, nasturtiums, comfrey, borage, chamomile, mint, tansy, lavender, rosemary, thyme, sage, marigolds, carrots, beets, spinach, peas, beans, lettuce.
These plants deter pests and attract beneficial insects.
- **Bad Companions**: Potatoes, tomatoes, cabbage family, fennel, black walnut.

Nightshades can spread diseases, and cabbage-family plants compete for nutrients.
- **Additional Notes**:
    - Plant **marigolds** and **nasturtiums** around cherry trees to deter pests.
    - Avoid planting near **walnut trees**, as they release juglone.
    - Prune cherry trees regularly to improve air circulation.

Cranberry

- **Good Companions**: Blueberries, huckleberries, strawberries, heather, pine trees, oak trees, azaleas, rhododendrons, clover, lupine, legumes (beans, peas), mustard greens, radishes, carrots, beets, lettuce, spinach, dill, chamomile, yarrow, mint.
  These plants thrive in acidic soil and attract beneficial insects.
- **Bad Companions**: Cabbage family, tomatoes, potatoes, peppers, eggplant, cucumbers, melons.
  Cabbage-family plants compete for nutrients, and nightshades can spread diseases.
- **Additional Notes**:
    - Cranberries prefer acidic soil (pH 4.0–5.5). Use peat moss or sand to maintain acidity.
    - Plant **clover** or **lupine** nearby to fix nitrogen in the soil.
    - Avoid planting near **walnut trees**, as they release juglone.

Grapes

- **Good Companions**: Basil, oregano, marigolds, lavender, clover, rosemary, sage, thyme, chamomile, dill, yarrow, nasturtiums, carrots, beets, lettuce, spinach, peas, beans.
  These plants deter pests and attract beneficial insects.
- **Bad Companions**: Cabbage, broccoli, Brussels sprouts, fennel, black walnut, potatoes, tomatoes.
  Cabbage-family plants compete for nutrients, and nightshades can spread diseases.
- **Additional Notes**:

- Plant **marigolds** and **nasturtiums** around grapevines to deter pests.
- Avoid planting near **walnut trees**, as they release juglone.
- Prune grapevines regularly to improve air circulation.

Gooseberry

- **Good Companions**: Garlic, chives, marigolds, nasturtiums, chamomile, borage, comfrey, lavender, rosemary, thyme, sage, carrots, beets, spinach, lettuce, peas, beans.
  These plants deter pests and attract beneficial insects.
- **Bad Companions**: Fennel, black walnut, cabbage family.
  Fennel and black walnut inhibit gooseberry growth, and cabbage-family plants compete for nutrients.
- **Additional Notes**:
  - Plant **marigolds** and **nasturtiums** around gooseberry bushes to deter pests.
  - Avoid planting near **walnut trees**, as they release juglone.
  - Prune gooseberry bushes regularly to improve air circulation.

Honeyberry

- **Good Companions**: Strawberries, clover, lupine, azaleas, rhododendrons, legumes (beans, peas), mustard greens, radishes, carrots, beets, lettuce, spinach, dill, chamomile, yarrow, mint.
  These plants thrive in acidic soil and attract beneficial insects.
- **Bad Companions**: Cabbage family, tomatoes, potatoes, peppers, eggplant, cucumbers, melons.
  Cabbage-family plants compete for nutrients, and nightshades can spread diseases.
- **Additional Notes**:
  - Honeyberries prefer acidic soil (pH 5.0–6.0). Use pine needles or oak leaves as mulch to maintain acidity.
  - Plant **clover** or **lupine** nearby to fix nitrogen in the soil.

- Avoid planting near **walnut trees**, as they release juglone.

Jostaberry

- **Good Companions**: Garlic, chives, marigolds, nasturtiums, chamomile, borage, comfrey, lavender, rosemary, thyme, sage, carrots, beets, spinach, lettuce, peas, beans.
  These plants deter pests and attract beneficial insects.
- **Bad Companions**: Fennel, black walnut, cabbage family.
  Fennel and black walnut inhibit jostaberry growth, and cabbage-family plants compete for nutrients.
- **Additional Notes**:
  - Plant **marigolds** and **nasturtiums** around jostaberry bushes to deter pests.
  - Avoid planting near **walnut trees**, as they release juglone.
  - Prune jostaberry bushes regularly to improve air circulation.

Kiwi

- **Good Companions**: Nasturtiums, comfrey, borage, lavender, chamomile, mint, tansy, marigolds, carrots, beets, spinach, peas, beans, lettuce, rosemary, sage, thyme, chives, garlic, clover, dill, yarrow.
  These plants deter pests and attract beneficial insects.
- **Bad Companions**: Potatoes, tomatoes, cabbage family, fennel, black walnut.
  Nightshades can spread diseases, and cabbage-family plants compete for nutrients.
- **Additional Notes**:
  - Plant **marigolds** and **nasturtiums** around kiwi vines to deter pests.
  - Avoid planting near **walnut trees**, as they release juglone.
  - Prune kiwi vines regularly to improve air circulation.

Loganberry

- **Good Companions**: Marigolds, nasturtiums, garlic, chives, dill, chamomile, thyme, borage, lavender, parsley, rosemary, sage, mint, tansy, comfrey, clover, yarrow, potatoes, asparagus, rhubarb, lettuce, spinach, carrots, beets, peas, beans.
  These plants deter pests and attract beneficial insects.
- **Bad Companions**: Potatoes, tomatoes, peppers, eggplant, cucumbers, melons, squash, fennel, black walnut, cabbage family.
  Nightshades can spread diseases, and cabbage-family plants compete for nutrients.
- **Additional Notes**:
  - Plant **marigolds** and **nasturtiums** around loganberry bushes to deter pests.
  - Avoid planting near **walnut trees**, as they release juglone.
  - Prune loganberry bushes regularly to improve air circulation.

Pear

- **Good Companions**: Chives, garlic, clover, dill, yarrow, nasturtiums, comfrey, borage, chamomile, mint, tansy, lavender, rosemary, thyme, sage, marigolds, carrots, beets, spinach, peas, beans, lettuce.
  These plants deter pests and attract beneficial insects.
- **Bad Companions**: Potatoes, tomatoes, cabbage family, fennel, black walnut.
  Nightshades can spread diseases, and cabbage-family plants compete for nutrients.
- **Additional Notes**:
  - Plant **marigolds** and **nasturtiums** around pear trees to deter pests.
  - Avoid planting near **walnut trees**, as they release juglone.
  - Prune pear trees regularly to improve air circulation.

Physalis (Cape Gooseberry)

- **Good Companions**: Borage, thyme, marigolds, nasturtiums, basil, oregano, rosemary, sage, carrots, beets, lettuce, spinach, peas, beans.
  These plants deter pests and attract beneficial insects.
- **Bad Companions**: Potatoes, tomatoes, peppers, eggplant, cucumbers, melons, squash, fennel, black walnut, cabbage family.
  Nightshades can spread diseases, and cabbage-family plants compete for nutrients.
- **Additional Notes**:
  - Plant **marigolds** and **nasturtiums** around physalis plants to deter pests.
  - Avoid planting near **walnut trees**, as they release juglone.
  - Harvest physalis fruits when the husks turn papery and dry.

Plum

- **Good Companions**: Chives, garlic, clover, dill, yarrow, nasturtiums, comfrey, borage, chamomile, mint, tansy, lavender, rosemary, thyme, sage, marigolds, carrots, beets, spinach, peas, beans, lettuce.
  These plants deter pests and attract beneficial insects.
- **Bad Companions**: Potatoes, tomatoes, cabbage family, fennel, black walnut.
  Nightshades can spread diseases, and cabbage-family plants compete for nutrients.
- **Additional Notes**:
  - Plant **marigolds** and **nasturtiums** around plum trees to deter pests.
  - Avoid planting near **walnut trees**, as they release juglone.
  - Prune plum trees regularly to improve air circulation.

Quince

- **Good Companions**: Chives, garlic, clover, dill, yarrow, nasturtiums, comfrey, borage, chamomile, mint, tansy, lavender, rosemary, thyme, sage, marigolds, carrots, beets, spinach, peas, beans, lettuce.
  These plants deter pests and attract beneficial insects.
- **Bad Companions**: Potatoes, tomatoes, cabbage family, fennel, black walnut.
  Nightshades can spread diseases, and cabbage-family plants compete for nutrients.
- **Additional Notes**:
    - Plant **marigolds** and **nasturtiums** around quince trees to deter pests.
    - Avoid planting near **walnut trees**, as they release juglone.
    - Prune quince trees regularly to improve air circulation.

Raspberry

- **Good Companions**: Marigolds, nasturtiums, garlic, chives, dill, chamomile, thyme, borage, lavender, parsley, rosemary, sage, mint, tansy, comfrey, clover, yarrow, potatoes, asparagus, rhubarb, lettuce, spinach, carrots, beets, peas, beans.
  These plants deter pests and attract beneficial insects.
- **Bad Companions**: Potatoes, tomatoes, peppers, eggplant, cucumbers, melons, squash, fennel, black walnut, cabbage family.
  Nightshades can spread diseases, and cabbage-family plants compete for nutrients.
- **Additional Notes**:
    - Plant **marigolds** and **nasturtiums** around raspberry bushes to deter pests.
    - Avoid planting near **walnut trees**, as they release juglone.
    - Prune raspberry bushes regularly to improve air circulation.

Redcurrant

- **Good Companions**: Garlic, chives, marigolds, nasturtiums, chamomile, borage, comfrey, lavender, rosemary, thyme, sage, carrots, beets, spinach, lettuce, peas, beans.
  These plants deter pests and attract beneficial insects.
- **Bad Companions**: Fennel, black walnut, cabbage family. Fennel and black walnut inhibit redcurrant growth, and cabbage-family plants compete for nutrients.
- **Additional Notes**:
  - Plant **marigolds** and **nasturtiums** around redcurrant bushes to deter pests.
  - Avoid planting near **walnut trees**, as they release juglone.
  - Prune redcurrant bushes regularly to improve air circulation.

Strawberry

- **Good Companions**: Borage, thyme, bush beans, lettuce, spinach, garlic, onions, dill, chamomile, carrots, parsley, marigolds, rosemary, sage, lavender, chives, beets, radishes.
  These plants deter pests and attract beneficial insects.
- **Bad Companions**: Cabbage family, potatoes, tomatoes, peppers, eggplant, cucumbers, melons, squash.
  Cabbage-family plants compete for nutrients, and nightshades can spread diseases.
- **Additional Notes**:
  - Plant **marigolds** and **nasturtiums** around strawberry plants to deter pests.
  - Avoid planting near **walnut trees**, as they release juglone.
  - Mulch around strawberry plants to retain moisture and suppress weeds.

Tayberry

- **Good Companions**: Marigolds, nasturtiums, garlic, chives, dill, chamomile, thyme, borage, lavender, parsley, rosemary, sage, mint, tansy, comfrey, clover, yarrow, potatoes, asparagus, rhubarb, lettuce, spinach, carrots, beets, peas, beans.
  These plants deter pests and attract beneficial insects.
- **Bad Companions**: Potatoes, tomatoes, peppers, eggplant, cucumbers, melons, squash, fennel, black walnut, cabbage family.
  Nightshades can spread diseases, and cabbage-family plants compete for nutrients.
- **Additional Notes**:
  - Plant **marigolds** and **nasturtiums** around tayberry bushes to deter pests.
  - Avoid planting near **walnut trees**, as they release juglone.
  - Prune tayberry bushes regularly to improve air circulation.

Thornless Blackberry

- **Good Companions**: Marigolds, nasturtiums, garlic, chives, dill, chamomile, thyme, borage, lavender, parsley, rosemary, sage, mint, tansy, comfrey, clover, yarrow, potatoes, asparagus, rhubarb, lettuce, spinach, carrots, beets, peas, beans.
  These plants deter pests and attract beneficial insects.
- **Bad Companions**: Potatoes, tomatoes, peppers, eggplant, cucumbers, melons, squash, fennel, black walnut, cabbage family.
  Nightshades can spread diseases, and cabbage-family plants compete for nutrients.
- **Additional Notes**:
  - Plant **marigolds** and **nasturtiums** around thornless blackberry bushes to deter pests.
  - Avoid planting near **walnut trees**, as they release juglone.

- Prune thornless blackberry bushes regularly to improve air circulation.

Wintergreen

- **Good Companions**: Blueberries, cranberries, huckleberries, strawberries, heather, pine trees, oak trees, azaleas, rhododendrons, clover, lupine, legumes (beans, peas), mustard greens, radishes, carrots, beets, lettuce, spinach, dill, chamomile, yarrow, mint.
  These plants thrive in acidic soil and attract beneficial insects.
- **Bad Companions**: Cabbage family, tomatoes, potatoes, peppers, eggplant, cucumbers, melons.
  Cabbage-family plants compete for nutrients, and nightshades can spread diseases.
- **Additional Notes**:
  - Wintergreen prefers acidic soil (pH 4.5–5.5). Use pine needles or oak leaves as mulch to maintain acidity.
  - Plant **clover** or **lupine** nearby to fix nitrogen in the soil.
  - Avoid planting near **walnut trees**, as they release juglone.

The Magic of Herbs

Herbs are the unsung heroes of the garden, playing dual roles as culinary staples and defenders against pests. One of the joys of growing perennial herbs is their year-round presence in the garden. Even when other plants are dormant, you can snip a sprig of rosemary or gather winter savory to brighten up your winter cooking. Many of these hardy herbs thrive in less-than-ideal soils, making them perfect for those tricky spots where other plants struggle. Most perennial herbs are evergreen or reliably return each year. To keep them bushy and productive, harvest up to a third of their growth annually. Many also adapt well to pots and containers, allowing you to bring them indoors for extra protection during harsh winters. Just remember that some perennial herbs, especially those from the Mediterranean, may not survive winters colder than USDA hardiness zone 8, so plan accordingly! Let's look at a few herbs and the many roles they play.

Thyme
This aromatic herb is not only a staple in the kitchen, transforming dishes with its fragrant leaves, but it also acts as a guardian for brussels sprouts. When planted together, thyme can deter pests like **Whiteflies,** cabbage worms, Tomato hornworms, and aphids, creating a healthier environment for your brussel sprout plants to thrive. This natural partnership doesn't just protect your crops; it also enriches the flavors of your homegrown produce, making every meal a celebration of fresh, vibrant tastes.

Mint
Mint, with its refreshing aroma, is another versatile herb that can offer substantial benefits. When paired with cabbage, mint helps repel cabbage moths and other common pests, reducing the need for chemical interventions. However, mint's vigorous growth can easily take over if not managed properly, so it's wise to plant it in a container or a designated border area. This way, you can enjoy its protective benefits without worrying about it overshadowing its companions. The partnership between mint and cabbage not only promotes a

healthy garden but provides a steady supply of fresh mint for teas, garnishes, and culinary experiments.

Dill

Dill is another herb worth incorporating into your garden, especially when planted alongside cucumbers. It aids in pest resistance by attracting beneficial insects like ladybugs, which feast on aphids and other pests that might threaten your plants. This natural form of pest control aligns perfectly with sustainable gardening practices, reducing reliance on pesticides. Dill's feathery leaves also add a touch of elegance to the garden, making it a feast for the eyes as well as the palate. The combination of dill and cucumbers is a classic example of how companion planting can enhance both garden health and culinary experiences, providing ingredients for pickles and salads straight from your backyard.

Companion Planting Guide for Herbs

Mix your favorite herbs with fruits or vegetables to create an aromatic and colorful blend of plants. Here are some combinations you can try

Anise

- **Annual or Perennial?** Annual
- **Good Companions**: Cabbage, coriander.
  Anise improves the growth and flavor of cabbage and coriander.
- **Bad Companions**: Basil, rosemary, thyme.
  These herbs can inhibit the growth of anise.
- **Additional Notes**:
    - Anise attracts beneficial insects like parasitic wasps.
    - Plant in well-drained soil and full sun.
    - Harvest seeds when they turn brown and dry.

Arugula/Rocket

- **Annual or Perennial?** Annual
- **Good Companions**: Carrots, radishes, garlic.
  Arugula grows well with carrots and radishes, and garlic deters pests like flea beetles.
- **Bad Companions**: Thyme.
  Thyme can inhibit the growth of arugula.
- **Additional Notes**:
    - Arugula is a fast-growing crop and can be used as a trap crop for pests.
    - Plant in cool weather to prevent bolting.
    - Harvest leaves when they are young and tender.

Basil

- **Annual or Perennial?**: Annual, Perennial in Zones 10+
- **Good Companions**: Tomatoes, peppers, asparagus, oregano, cabbage, rosemary, marigolds.
  Basil improves the flavor of tomatoes and peppers and repels pests like aphids and whiteflies.
- **Bad Companions**: Rue.
  Rue can inhibit the growth of basil.
- **Additional Notes**:
    - Basil thrives in warm, well-drained soil and benefits from regular pruning.
    - Use basil as a natural pest deterrent in the garden.
    - Harvest leaves before the plant flowers for the best flavor.

Bay Laurel

- **Annual or Perennial?**: Perennial
- **Good Companions**: Rosemary, sage, thyme.
  Bay laurel grows well with other Mediterranean herbs and can be used as a general pest deterrent.
- **Bad Companions**: None significant.
- **Additional Notes**:
    - Bay laurel prefers well-drained soil and full sun.

- Can be grown in containers in cooler climates.
- Harvest leaves as needed for culinary use.

Borage

- **Annual or Perennial?**: Annual
- **Good Companions**: Strawberries, tomatoes, squash, cabbage, marigolds.
  Borage deters pests like tomato hornworms and improves the flavor of strawberries.
- **Bad Companions**: None significant.
- **Additional Notes**:
  - Borage attracts pollinators like bees and is a dynamic accumulator, enriching the soil with nutrients.
  - Plant in well-drained soil and full sun.
  - Harvest flowers and leaves for culinary use.

Calendula

- **Annual or Perennial?**: Annual
- **Good Companions**: Tomatoes, cabbage, rosemary, thyme.
  Calendula deters pests like aphids and attracts beneficial insects like ladybugs.
- **Bad Companions**: None significant.
- **Additional Notes**:
  - Calendula is easy to grow and thrives in most soil types.
  - Use as a trap crop for pests.
  - Harvest flowers for medicinal and culinary use.

Chamomile

- **Annual or Perennial?**: Annual
- **Good Companions**: Cabbage, onions, broccoli, kale, basil, rosemary.
  Chamomile improves the flavor of cabbage and onions and attracts beneficial insects like hoverflies.
- **Bad Companions**: None significant.
- **Additional Notes**:

- Chamomile prefers well-drained soil and full sun.
- Used to make a natural insect repellent spray.
- Harvest flowers for tea and medicinal use.

Chervil

- **Annual or Perennial?**: Annual
- **Good Companions**: Lettuce, radishes.
  Chervil improves the growth and flavor of lettuce and radishes.
- **Bad Companions**: None significant.
- **Additional Notes**:
    - Chervil prefers partial shade and moist soil.
    - Attracts beneficial insects like hoverflies.
    - Harvest leaves when they are young and tender.

Chives

- **Annual or Perennial?**: Perennial
- **Good Companions**: Carrots, tomatoes, strawberries, roses, fruit trees, lettuce, beets, cabbage, garlic, marigolds.
  Chives deter pests like aphids and improve the flavor of carrots and tomatoes.
- **Bad Companions**: Beans, peas.
  Chives can inhibit the growth of legumes.
- **Additional Notes**:
    - Chives are easy to grow and thrive in most soil types.
    - Use as a natural pest deterrent in the garden.
    - Harvest leaves as needed for culinary use.

Cilantro/Coriander

- **Annual or Perennial?**: Annual
- **Good Companions**: Carrots, potatoes, spinach, dill.
  Cilantro deters pests like aphids and spider mites and improves the growth of spinach and lettuce.
- **Bad Companions**: Fennel.
  Fennel can inhibit the growth of cilantro.
- **Additional Notes**:

- Cilantro prefers cool weather and well-drained soil.
- Attracts beneficial insects like hoverflies.
- Harvest leaves before the plant flowers for the best flavor.

Dill

- **Annual or Perennial?**: Annual
- **Good Companions**: Cabbage, cucumbers, lettuce, onions. Dill attracts beneficial insects like ladybugs and improves the growth of cabbage and lettuce.
- **Bad Companions**: Carrots, tomatoes. Dill can inhibit the growth of carrots and attract pests harmful to tomatoes.
- **Additional Notes**:
  - Dill prefers well-drained soil and full sun.
  - Use as a trap crop for pests.
  - Harvest leaves and seeds for culinary use.

Flax

- **Annual or Perennial?**: Annual
- **Good Companions**: Carrots, potatoes. Flax improves the growth of carrots and potatoes and attracts beneficial insects.
- **Bad Companions**: None significant.
- **Additional Notes**:
  - Flax prefers well-drained soil and full sun.
  - Use as a cover crop to improve soil health.
  - Harvest seeds for culinary and medicinal use.

Garlic Chives

- **Annual or Perennial?**: Perennial
- **Good Companions**: Carrots, tomatoes, strawberries, roses, fruit trees, lettuce, beets, cabbage, garlic, marigolds. Garlic chives deter pests like aphids and improve the flavor of carrots and tomatoes.

- **Bad Companions**: Beans, peas.
  Garlic chives can inhibit the growth of legumes.
- **Additional Notes**:
    - Garlic chives are easy to grow and thrive in most soil types.
    - Use as a natural pest deterrent in the garden.
    - Harvest leaves as needed for culinary use.

Lavender

- **Annual or Perennial?**: Perennial
- **Good Companions**: Cabbage, rosemary, thyme, garlic, beets, carrots, kale, marigolds, chamomile, oregano, basil. Lavender deters pests like moths and fleas and attracts pollinators like bees.
- **Bad Companions**: Fennel, mint (can be invasive and compete), rue.
  These herbs can inhibit the growth of lavender.
- **Additional Notes**:
    - Lavender prefers well-drained soil and full sun.
    - Used to make a natural insect repellent spray.
    - Harvest flowers for culinary and medicinal use.

Lemon Balm

- **Annual or Perennial?**: Perennial
- **Good Companions**: Tomatoes, cabbage, broccoli. Lemon balm deters pests like squash bugs and attracts beneficial insects like bees.
- **Bad Companions**: None significant.
- **Additional Notes**:
    - Lemon balm prefers moist soil and partial shade.
    - Can be invasive, so plant in containers if necessary.
    - Harvest leaves for tea and medicinal use.

Lemon Verbena

- **Annual or Perennial?**: Perennial
- **Good Companions**: Rosemary, sage, thyme.
  Lemon verbena deters pests like whiteflies and improves the flavor of tomatoes and peppers.
- **Bad Companions**: None significant.
- **Additional Notes**:
  - Lemon verbena prefers well-drained soil and full sun.
  - Used to make a natural insect repellent spray.
  - Harvest leaves for tea and culinary use.

Lovage

- **Annual or Perennial?**: Perennial
- **Good Companions**: Beans, peas, potatoes, tomatoes, lettuce, rosemary, sage, borage.
  Lovage improves the growth of beans and peas and attracts beneficial insects.
- **Bad Companions**: Fennel.
  Fennel can inhibit the growth of lovage.
- **Additional Notes**:
  - Lovage prefers moist soil and partial shade.
  - Use as a natural pest deterrent in the garden.
  - Harvest leaves and stems for culinary use.

Marjoram

- **Annual or Perennial?**: Perennial
- **Good Companions**: Beans, cabbage, rosemary, thyme, oregano.
  Marjoram improves the flavor of nearby plants and attracts beneficial insects like bees.
- **Bad Companions**: Cucumbers.
  Cucumbers can inhibit the growth of marjoram.
- **Additional Notes**:
  - Marjoram prefers well-drained soil and full sun.
  - Use as a natural pest deterrent in the garden.
  - Harvest leaves for culinary use.

Mint

- **Annual or Perennial?**: Perennial
- **Good Companions**: Cabbage, tomatoes, broccoli, kale, carrots, beets, lavender, thyme, rosemary.
  Mint deters pests like aphids and cabbage moths.
- **Bad Companions**: Cucumbers, parsley, dill.
  Mint can inhibit the growth of these plants.
- **Additional Notes**:
  - Mint is invasive and should be grown in containers to prevent it from spreading.
  - Use as a natural pest deterrent in the garden.
  - Harvest leaves for tea and culinary use.

Mustard

- **Annual or Perennial?**: Annual
- **Good Companions**: Beans, peas.
  Mustard attracts beneficial insects and can be used as a cover crop to improve soil health.
- **Bad Companions**: None significant.
- **Additional Notes**:
  - Mustard prefers well-drained soil and full sun.
  - Use as a trap crop for pests.
  - Harvest leaves and seeds for culinary use.

Nasturtium

- **Annual or Perennial?**: Annual
- **Good Companions**: Cabbage, tomatoes, cucumbers, fruit trees.
  Nasturtium deters pests like aphids and attracts beneficial insects like hoverflies.
- **Bad Companions**: None significant.
- **Additional Notes**:
  - Nasturtium is easy to grow and thrives in most soil types.
  - Use as a trap crop for pests.
  - Harvest flowers and leaves for culinary use.

Oregano

- **Annual or Perennial?**: Perennial
- **Good Companions**: Beans, cabbage, rosemary, thyme, lavender, basil, tomatoes, peppers.
  Oregano deters pests like aphids and improves the flavor of nearby plants.
- **Bad Companions**: Cucumbers, fennel.
  These plants can inhibit the growth of oregano.
- **Additional Notes**:
  - Oregano prefers well-drained soil and full sun.
  - Use as a natural pest deterrent in the garden.
  - Harvest leaves for culinary use.

Rosemary

- **Annual or Perennial?**: Perennial
- **Good Companions**: Cabbage, carrots, beans, sage, thyme, lavender, marigolds, borage, nasturtiums, garlic, chives.
  Rosemary deters pests like cabbage moths and bean beetles.
- **Bad Companions**: Cucumbers (some sources say cucumbers do well, but some do not, monitor), kohlrabi, sage, thyme, parsley, fennel.
  These plants can inhibit the growth of rosemary.
- **Additional Notes**:
  - Rosemary prefers well-drained soil and full sun.
  - Use as a natural pest deterrent in the garden.
  - Harvest leaves for culinary use.

Rue

- **Annual or Perennial?**: Perennial
- **Good Companions**: Roses, lavender.
  Rue deters pests like Japanese beetles and aphids.
- **Bad Companions**: Basil, sage, mint.
  These herbs can inhibit the growth of rue.
- **Additional Notes**:
  - Rue prefers well-drained soil and full sun.

- Can be toxic if ingested in large quantities.
  - Use as a natural pest deterrent in the garden.

Sage

- **Annual or Perennial?**: Perennial
- **Good Companions**: Rosemary, cabbage, carrots, strawberries, lavender, thyme.
  Sage deters pests like cabbage worms and carrot flies.
- **Bad Companions**: Cucumbers, fennel.
  These plants can inhibit the growth of sage.
- **Additional Notes**:
  - Sage prefers well-drained soil and full sun.
  - Use as a natural pest deterrent in the garden.
  - Harvest leaves for culinary use.

Salad Burnet

- **Annual or Perennial?**: Perennial
- **Good Companions**: Cabbage, rosemary, thyme, borage.
  Salad burnet attracts beneficial insects and improves the flavor of nearby plants.
- **Bad Companions**: None significant.
- **Additional Notes**:
  - Salad burnet prefers well-drained soil and full sun.
  - Use as a natural pest deterrent in the garden.
  - Harvest leaves for culinary use.

Summer Savory

- **Annual or Perennial?**: Annual
- **Good Companions**: Beans, cabbage, rosemary, thyme.
  Summer savory improves the growth and flavor of beans and cabbage.
- **Bad Companions**: None significant.
- **Additional Notes**:
  - Summer savory prefers well-drained soil and full sun.
  - Use as a natural pest deterrent in the garden.
  - Harvest leaves for culinary use.

Sweet Cicely

- **Annual or Perennial?**: Perennial
- **Good Companions**: Rosemary, sage, thyme, lovage.
  Sweet cicely attracts beneficial insects and improves the flavor of nearby plants.
- **Bad Companions**: None significant.
- **Additional Notes**:
  - Sweet cicely prefers moist soil and partial shade.
  - Use as a natural pest deterrent in the garden.
  - Harvest leaves and seeds for culinary use.

Tarragon

- **Annual or Perennial?**: Perennial
- **Good Companions**: Cabbage, tomatoes, peppers, eggplant, rosemary, thyme, borage.
  Tarragon improves the flavor of nearby plants and deters pests like aphids.
- **Bad Companions**: None significant.
- **Additional Notes**:
  - Tarragon prefers well-drained soil and full sun.
  - Use as a natural pest deterrent in the garden.
  - Harvest leaves for culinary use.

Thyme

- **Annual or Perennial?**: Perennial
- **Good Companions**: Cabbage, strawberries, tomatoes, potatoes, rosemary, lavender, garlic, beets, marigolds, nasturtiums, oregano, basil.
  Thyme deters pests like cabbage worms and improves the flavor of nearby plants.
- **Bad Companions**: Cucumber, arugula, fennel.
  These plants can inhibit the growth of thyme.
- **Additional Notes**:
  - Thyme prefers well-drained soil and full sun.
  - Use as a natural pest deterrent in the garden.
  - Harvest leaves for culinary use.

Winter Savory

- **Annual or Perennial?**: Perennial
- **Good Companions**: Beans, cabbage, rosemary, thyme, oregano, garlic.
  Winter savory improves the growth and flavor of beans and cabbage.
- **Bad Companions**: Cucumbers.
  Cucumbers can inhibit the growth of winter savory.
- **Additional Notes**:
  - Winter savory prefers well-drained soil and full sun.
  - Use as a natural pest deterrent in the garden.
  - Harvest leaves for culinary use.

Pest Repelling Herbs

Incorporating pest-repelling herbs into your garden is a foolproof method to protect your plants from unwanted visitors. These herbs release natural compounds that deter various insects and pests, reducing the need for chemical interventions. Strategically planting these herbs throughout your garden creates a healthier and more balanced ecosystem, promoting plant growth and minimizing pest damage. Below is a list of herbs known for their pest-deterrent properties, along with the specific pests they help to keep away.

- **Basil**: Deters flies, mosquitoes, flea beetles, and cabbage webworms. The oil in basil kills mosquito eggs
- **Lavender**: Repels mosquitoes, moths, fleas, and flies.
- **Mint**: Repels moths, ants, beetles, fleas, mice, mosquitoes, and aphids.
- **Rosemary**: Repels slugs, beetles, and mosquitoes.
- **Chives**: Stave off aphids, mites, carrot flies, and Japanese beetles, and also keep away rabbits while attracting pollinators when they flower.
- **Dill**: Repels aphids and spider mites.

- **Alliums** (including leeks, chives, and shallots): Repel aphids, cabbage worms, slugs, and carrot flies.
- **Catnip**: Repels mosquitoes and other insects.
- **Lemongrass**: Contains citronella and repels insects.
- **Oregano**: Deters certain pests and insects, such as the cabbage butterfly and the cucumber beetle.
- **Thyme**: Deters mosquitoes, earworm, maggot, hornworm, and whiteflies.

Border Planting

To integrate these herbs effectively, consider using border planting techniques. Herbs can form a natural boundary around vegetable beds, offering protection and enhancing aesthetics.

Many herbs can create a natural boundary around vegetable garden beds, offering practical, low-maintenance, and edible edging solutions. They serve to define boundaries while enhancing the garden's features. When selecting herbs for edging, it's important to consider their mature height, usefulness, fragrance, and color.

Here are some herbs suitable for creating a border:
- **Sage** - With its bushy growth habit, sage makes an excellent border plant for vegetable beds and attracts pollinators when it's flowering. Plant it near brassicas, carrots, lettuce, and beans to deter pests such as cabbage moth and carrot fly. It thrives alongside lavender, lemon balm, lemon thyme, lemon verbena, lovage, oregano, parsley, rosemary, savory, thyme, and tarragon.
- **Thyme** - If the border is at risk of being trampled on, thyme is a good choice because it can take a beating.
- **Rosemary** - Planted alongside other herbs like sage, thyme, oregano, and lavender, it enhances growth and repels pests.
- **Lavender** - Pairs well with rosemary, thyme, oregano, and sage and can create a beautiful, fragrant herb garden together.

- **Marjoram** - It is a friend to all plants and helps improve growth and flavor.
- **Other herbs** - Basil, calendula, chamomile, cilantro, dill, fennel, feverfew, hyssop, nasturtium, purple coneflower, and scented geraniums.

To create an herb border, it's best to place low-growing plants in the front, tall ones in the back; however, you can mix things up to enhance aesthetic appeal if you prefer An herb border provides year-round flowers, mineral-rich foliage for mulching, and a never-ending supply of herbs for cooking and medicinal use.

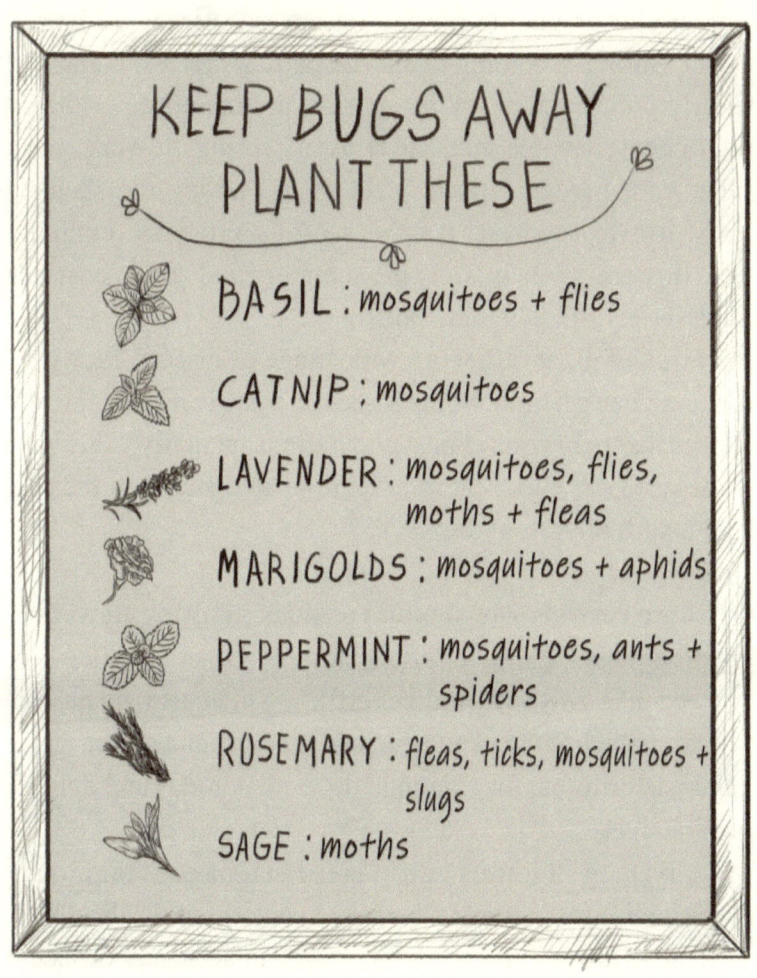

The Role of Flowers in Companion Planting

Flowers play a vital role in companion planting by attracting pollinators, controlling pests, improving soil health, and enhancing biodiversity, ultimately creating a healthier and more productive garden ecosystem. Flowers are much more than decorative touches in a garden; they are crucial contributors to its health and vitality. Their vibrant blooms do more than just please the eye—they invite pollinators like bees, butterflies, and hummingbirds, essential visitors that facilitate the reproduction of many plants. This process not only boosts fruit and vegetable yields but ensures your garden remains a buzzing hub of life.

Timing your flower plantings can make a significant difference in their impact. Spring-blooming plants are particularly valuable, as they provide early pollen and nectar sources for pollinators emerging from winter dormancy. By planting an array of spring flowers, you can ensure that your garden attracts plant allies, setting the stage for a productive growing season. As the seasons progress, continue to introduce flowers that bloom in summer and fall, ensuring a continuous supply of nectar and pollen.

A diverse array of plants attracts a wide range of insects, each playing a role in the garden's health. Some insects are pollinators, while others are predators that help control pest populations naturally. This balance reduces the need for chemical interventions and supports the overall ecological health of your garden.

Here are some reasons you should consider planting flowers:

- Natural Pest Control - Certain flowers attract beneficial insects like ladybugs and hoverflies, which prey on harmful pests, reducing the need for chemical pesticides. Marigolds and nasturtiums, for example, deter nematodes and aphids, respectively.
- Biodiversity - Flowers attract beneficial insects, birds, and other wildlife, creating a balanced ecosystem. Pollinator-friendly flowers like bee balm and echinacea support bees and butterflies, ensuring plant reproduction.

- <u>Enhanced Growth</u> - Flowers like marigolds improve soil health, while nitrogen-fixing plants such as sweet peas enrich the soil for neighboring plants. Taller flowers can create beneficial microclimates, providing shade and reducing water evaporation.
- <u>Improved Soil Health</u> - Specific plants can significantly improve soil quality, promoting healthier growth for all nearby plants. Borage adds trace minerals to the soil and helps improve soil structure with its deep roots.
- <u>Attracting Pollinators</u> - Growing a flowering plant can attract pollinating insects, which are needed for fruit onset.

Companion Planting Guide for Flowers

Flowers in the garden aren't just pretty to look at, they play crucial roles in attracting pollinators, warding off pests, and keeping the garden healthy and flourishing. You can maximize their benefits by pairing them with fruits, vegetables, and herbs that they like the most. Here's a chart detailing some beneficial flower pairings:

Alyssum

- **Good Companions**: Grapes, lettuce.
  Alyssum attracts beneficial pollinators like bees and hoverflies, which help with the pollination of grapes and lettuce.
- **Benefits**:
  - Alyssum is a low-growing flower that provides ground cover, helping to retain soil moisture and suppress weeds.
  - It is particularly effective in attracting parasitic wasps, which prey on aphids and other pests.
- **Additional Notes**:
  - Plant alyssum around the base of grapevines or in lettuce beds for optimal benefits.
  - Alyssum thrives in well-drained soil and full sun to partial shade.

Borage

- **Good Companions**: Almost everything, especially beans, strawberries, cucumbers, squash, fruit trees, tomatoes, and cabbage.
  Borage is a versatile companion plant that benefits a wide range of vegetables and fruits.
- **Benefits**:
  - Borage adds trace minerals to the soil, particularly calcium and potassium, which are essential for plant growth.
  - Its deep roots help improve soil structure and aeration.

- o Borage attracts pollinators like bees and beneficial insects like hoverflies.
- **Additional Notes**:
    - o Plant borage near tomatoes to improve their growth and flavor.
    - o Borage is also known to deter tomato hornworms and cabbage worms.
    - o Harvest borage flowers for culinary use or to make a natural pest repellent spray.

Calendula

- **Good Companions**: Nearly all plants, particularly peppers, tomatoes, cucumbers, squash, potatoes, roses, alliums, and brassicas.
Calendula is a versatile flower that benefits a wide range of plants.
- **Benefits**:
    - o Calendula attracts beneficial insects like ladybugs and hoverflies, which prey on aphids and other pests.
    - o It can also act as a trap crop, attracting pests away from more valuable plants.
    - o Calendula has antifungal properties that can help prevent soil-borne diseases.
- **Additional Notes**:
    - o Plant calendula around the base of tomatoes and peppers to deter pests and improve soil health.
    - o Calendula flowers can be harvested for medicinal use or to make a natural insect repellent spray.

Chamomile

- **Good Companions**: Cabbages and other brassicas, cucumbers, onions.
Chamomile is a beneficial companion for many vegetables.
- **Benefits**:
    - o Chamomile attracts beneficial insects like hoverflies and parasitic wasps, which prey on aphids and other pests.

- It can also improve the flavor of nearby plants, particularly cabbages and onions.
- Chamomile has antifungal properties that can help prevent soil-borne diseases.
- **Additional Notes**:
    - Plant chamomile near cabbages and cucumbers to deter pests and improve growth.
    - Harvest chamomile flowers for tea or to make a natural insect repellent spray.

Chrysanthemum

- **Good Companions**: Generally compatible with most plants, but can inhibit the growth of lettuce due to their allelopathic properties.
Chrysanthemums are known for their pest-repellent properties.
- **Benefits**:
    - Chrysanthemums contain pyrethrum, a natural insect repellent effective against ants, beetles, and other pests.
    - They can be used to make a natural insecticide spray.
- **Additional Notes**:
    - Plant chrysanthemums around the perimeter of the garden to deter pests.
    - Avoid planting near lettuce, as chrysanthemums can inhibit its growth.

Geraniums

- **Good Companions**: Roses, corn, peppers, and grapes.
Geraniums are effective at repelling certain pests.
- **Benefits**:
    - Geraniums repel pests like Japanese beetles and aphids, protecting nearby plants.
    - They also attract beneficial insects like hoverflies.
- **Additional Notes**:
    - Plant geraniums near roses, corn, and peppers to deter pests and improve growth.
    - Geraniums thrive in well-drained soil and full sun.

Lavender

- **Good Companions**: Generally compatible with most plants. Lavender is a versatile flower that benefits many plants.
- **Benefits**:
    - Lavender deters pests like mosquitoes, fleas, and moths, protecting nearby plants.
    - It attracts pollinators like bees and butterflies.
- **Additional Notes**:
    - Plant lavender around the perimeter of the garden or near vegetables like tomatoes and cabbage.
    - Lavender thrives in well-drained soil and full sun.

Lupin

- **Good Companions**: Brassicas, lettuces, rosemary, dill, strawberries, roses.
Lupins are beneficial for improving soil health.
- **Benefits**:
    - Lupins are nitrogen-fixing plants, enriching the soil with nitrogen and benefiting nearby plants.
    - They attract beneficial insects like bees and hoverflies.
- **Additional Notes**:
    - Plant lupins near brassicas and strawberries to improve soil health and deter pests.
    - Lupins prefer well-drained soil and full sun.

Marigold

- **Good Companions**: Nearly all plants, particularly peppers, tomatoes, cucumbers, squash, potatoes, roses, alliums, and brassicas.
Marigolds are one of the most popular companion plants.
- **Benefits**:
    - Marigolds suppress nematodes and other soil-borne pests, improving soil health.
    - They deter pests like aphids and whiteflies.
- **Additional Notes**:
    - Marigolds thrive in well-drained soil and full sun.

- Plant marigolds around the base of tomatoes, peppers, and cucumbers to deter pests and improve growth.

Nasturtium

- **Good Companions**: Beans, squash, tomatoes, fruit trees, brassicas, radishes, cucumbers.
  Nasturtiums are excellent trap crops and pest deterrents.
- **Benefits**:
  - Nasturtiums deter pests like aphids and whiteflies.
  - They can also act as a trap crop, attracting pests away from more valuable plants.
- **Additional Notes**:
  - Plant nasturtiums near tomatoes, cucumbers, and brassicas to deter pests.
  - Nasturtiums thrive in well-drained soil and full sun to partial shade.

Pansy

- **Good Companions**: Alliums, onions, roses.
  Pansies are beneficial for attracting pollinators.
- **Benefits**:
  - Pansies attract pollinators like bees and butterflies, benefiting nearby plants.
- **Additional Notes**:
  - Plant pansies near roses and alliums to improve pollination.
  - Pansies prefer well-drained soil and full sun to partial shade.

Petunia

- **Good Companions**: Squash, pumpkins, cucumbers, asparagus.
  Petunias are effective at repelling certain pests.
- **Benefits**:
  - Petunias repel pests like aphids and beetles, protecting nearby plants.
- **Additional Notes**:
  - Petunias thrive in well-drained soil and full sun.

- Plant petunias near squash, pumpkins, and cucumbers to deter pests.

Rose

- **Good Companions**: Chives, garlic, marigold.
  Roses benefit from pest-repellent companions.
- **Benefits**:
  - Garlic and chives deter pests like aphids and black spot, protecting roses.
  - Marigolds suppress nematodes and other soil-borne pests.
- **Additional Notes**:
  - Plant chives, garlic, and marigolds around the base of roses to deter pests and improve growth.
  - Roses prefer well-drained soil and full sun.

Sunflower

- **Good Companions**: Peppers, corn, soybeans, tomatoes, swan plants.
  Sunflowers are beneficial for attracting pollinators.
- **Benefits**:
  - Sunflowers attract pollinators like bees and beneficial insects like ladybugs.
  - They can also provide shade for heat-sensitive plants.
- **Additional Notes**:
  - Plant sunflowers near peppers and tomatoes to improve pollination.
  - Sunflowers thrive in well-drained soil and full sun.

Tansy

- **Good Companions**: Beans, brassicas, cucumbers, squash, raspberries, roses, corn, fruit trees.
  Tansy is effective at repelling certain pests.
- **Benefits**:
  - Tansy repels pests like ants, beetles, and flies, protecting nearby plants.

- **Additional Notes**:
    - Plant tansy around the perimeter of the garden or near fruit trees to deter pests.
    - Tansy prefers well-drained soil and full sun.

Interesting mixes

As a gardener, I swear by companion planting. Still, it took me some time to find the combinations that worked best for me and my plants. Here are some of my tried and tested planting mixes guaranteed to make gardening easy and more rewarding.

Chilies and Peppers

Enhance your urban garden with a vibrant mix of chili and sweet peppers. These compact, bushy plants first produce delicate white flowers, followed by fruits that ripen into stunning shades of orange, red, yellow, and purple. Pair them with golden marjoram and trailing Mexican daisies (Erigeron karvinskianus) for a striking display, as all three flourish in well-draining soil and abundant sunlight.

Here are the plants you'll need
1. Chili pepper "Numex Twilight"
2. Chili pepper "Fresno"
3. Sweet pepper "Sweet Banana"
4. Erigeron karvinskianus
5. Golden marjoram

Slowly adjust pepper and chili plants to outdoor conditions after the last frost before transplanting them. To improve drainage, place a layer of broken clay pot pieces over the drainage holes before adding compost. Water the soil whenever the surface feels dry and apply fertilizer every two weeks once the fruits begin to develop. Use stakes to support the plants and prevent them from drooping under the weight of the fruit.

Salads

In just six weeks, you'll be able to harvest a vibrant mix of salad leaves, edible flowers, and fragrant herbs from this setup. You can pick individual leaves from across the arrangement, allowing the plants to continue producing for weeks.

You'll need the following seeds for this combination
1. "Dazzle" lettuce
2. "Green Frills"
3. "Black Seeded Simpson" lettuce
4. 2 pots of marigolds (Calendula)
5. "Red Giant" mustard
6. Lemon thyme
7. Cosmos (optional)

Plant thyme and marigolds in mid-spring. Hold off on planting cosmos until the weather warms up. For Black Seeded Simpson lettuce, level the soil and sow the seeds thinly alongside mustard. Create diagonal sections and scatter purple and green lettuce seeds separately to keep them distinct. Finally, cover everything with a thin layer of compost and water thoroughly.

Mediterranean Tomato Pairings

This combination features a variety of tomatoes, including striped "Tigerellas", juicy cherry tomatoes, and sweet "Sungolds." Eggplants enhance both the beauty and productivity of this setup, while bright orange marigolds add a striking contrast.

Let's look at the plants that go into this exotic combination
- A pot of marigold (Calendula)
- Eggplant
- Sungold tomato
- Tigerella tomato
- Cherry tomato

Gradually acclimate young tomatoes and eggplants to outdoor conditions in late spring, ensuring proper drainage in their containers or raised beds. Support tomato plants with stakes and maintain consistent watering, keeping the soil from drying out. Once the first fruits appear, apply tomato fertilizer weekly to promote healthy growth.

Herb Mix

Hardy herbs are an excellent choice for beginners, as they offer a long harvesting season and are incredibly useful in the kitchen. While many herbs can thrive together, parsley is best grown separately since it tends to go to seed in its second year and may need replacing. A well-balanced mix includes thyme, marjoram, chives, and sage, complemented by trailing plants like brachyscome and petunias for added texture and color. Plant them in a sunny spot near the kitchen and fill the beds or containers with a high-quality, soil-based potting mix for optimal growth.

Here is a list of herbs that I like to plant together in my herb mix:
- Golden marjoram
- Parsley
- Variegated sage
- Bay
- Chives
- Golden lemon thyme

Plant herbs in the spring after the final frost. I prefer to tuck thyme and flowers into the side openings of a large herb pot while placing the remaining herbs on top. You can also create a smaller arrangement by pairing parsley with flowers. During the summer, keep the soil consistently moist, then reduce watering as temperatures cool.

The Signature Mix – Three Sisters

For centuries, indigenous peoples have practiced the Three Sisters method, a powerful example of companion planting. This mix includes three key components: corn, beans, and squash. The corn serves as the tallest plant in the trio and acts as a natural trellis for the climbing beans. It provides structural support, allowing beans to grow upward, which helps them reach sunlight more effectively. Beans are climbing plants that fix nitrogen in the soil through a symbiotic relationship with bacteria in their root nodules. This nitrogen enrichment benefits both the corn and the squash, enhancing soil fertility. The beans also help stabilize the corn stalks, making them less prone to damage from wind. Squash plants have broad leaves that spread out on the ground, creating a living mulch. This shading helps retain soil moisture and suppresses weeds. Additionally, some squash varieties have prickly stems or leaves that deter pests from approaching the other plants.

The Three Sisters are typically planted in mounds or clusters rather than in rows. Here's a general guide to planting them:
- Prepare Mounds - Create mounds of soil about 4-6 inches high and 18 inches wide, ensuring they receive full sunlight.
- Plant Corn First - Sow corn seeds in the center of each mound first, allowing it to establish height before other plants are added.
- Add Beans - Once the corn is about 6-8 inches tall, plant bean seeds around the corn stalks. The beans will climb up the corn as they grow.
- Include Squash Last - After the beans have emerged (about a week later), plant squash seeds around the perimeter of the mound to allow them space to spread out without overshadowing the younger corn and beans.

This staggered planting ensures that each sister has enough room and resources to thrive without competing directly with one another Grouping friendly plants is a shortcut to success in the garden. With the help of the charts and planting mixes above, you can steer clear of doomed combinations and go for the winning pairs. In the next chapter, we will look at common problems we may encounter while companion planting and how to overcome them.

CHAPTER 5

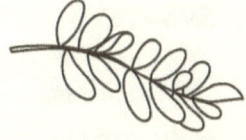

Troubleshooting and Common Pitfalls

When planning a garden, choosing the right plants for your climate and soil is not enough. It's important to understand how plants interact with one another. Their interactions, whether through roots, leaves, or seeds, can significantly impact your garden's success.

Take fennel, for example. It's a notorious troublemaker, releasing chemicals into the soil that most garden veggies find toxic. Imagine it as a neighbor who blasts loud music all day, making it hard for others to relax. To avoid stunted growth, keep fennel away from tomatoes, beans, and other sensitive plants. Instead, consider planting dill. Not only is it more cooperative, but it also attracts beneficial insects like ladybugs and lacewings, which help control pests like aphids.

Another common mistake is planting onions near peas or beans. Onions emit compounds that can hinder the growth of these plants, much like an overbearing friend who insists on doing things their way. If your pea plants look weak, have discolored leaves, or produce fewer peas than expected, nearby onions might be the culprit.

Signs Of Trouble

So, how can you tell if certain plants aren't getting along? Watch for signs like wilted leaves, slow growth, or an overall lack of vitality. These symptoms often indicate competition for soil nutrients and water—or one plant releasing chemicals that harm its neighbor. Sometimes, simply relocating a plant can solve the problem, giving it the space it needs to thrive.

How to Work Around Allelopathy in Companion Planting

Pairing the wrong plants together can cost us time, effort, and money. If you want to grow plants with allelopathic tendencies without harming your garden, don't lose hope, there are strategies to manage their effects.

- For example, you can grow vulnerable plants like tomatoes, beans, and carrots in raised beds or containers. This keeps them away from allelopathic plants like walnut trees or fennel, preventing harmful compounds from reaching their roots.
- Physical separation is also key. Keep allelopathic plants at least 5-10 feet (1.5-3 m) away from sensitive ones. For example, plant fennel in a dedicated herb bed rather than mixing it with your vegetable crops.
- Regular maintenance can make a big difference, too. Rake up fallen leaves to prevent toxins from seeping into the soil, and trim the flowers before they drop and inhibit nearby growth.
- Crop rotation is another effective tactic. Avoid planting sensitive crops in soil where allelopathic plants were previously grown. For instance, if broccoli occupied a bed last year, don't plant tomatoes there.
- Consider using buffer plants to neutralize allelopathic effects. Grasses like rye or wheat can absorb toxic compounds, while marigolds detoxify soil with their root secretions. Legumes

- such as clover, peas, and beans improve soil structure and help mitigate allelopathy.
- Improving soil health is also crucial. Allelopathic compounds break down faster in rich, well-aerated soil. Add compost, aged manure, or biochar to speed up the decomposition of harmful chemicals.
- Understanding which parts of a plant are allelopathic can help you plan better. For example, black walnuts release juglone mostly from their roots and leaves, so you can still grow plants in raised beds or containers nearby. Mint's allelopathic effects come from its aggressive roots, so planting it in containers prevents it from harming other herbs.
- If juglone or other allelopathic chemicals have built up in your soil, consider using cover crops to detoxify it. Buckwheat and mustard can help break down harmful compounds, while clover and alfalfa improve soil structure and fertility.
- Finally, timing your plantings can minimize allelopathic effects. Corn and sunflowers exhibit the most allelopathic tendencies during germination, so avoid planting sensitive crops near them during that time. Brassicas like cabbage and broccoli leave residues in the soil after harvesting, so wait a few weeks before replanting in those areas.

Common Allelopathic Plants

Here's a list of plants you should avoid to keep your garden thriving:

Black Walnut (Juglans nigra)
Black walnut trees release juglone, a toxic chemical that can stunt or kill sensitive plants like tomatoes, potatoes, peppers, apples, asparagus, and cabbage.

Broccoli & Cabbage (Brassicas)
Broccoli and cabbage release compounds into the soil that can slow the growth of solanaceous plants like tomatoes, peppers, and pole beans.

Chrysanthemums (Chrysanthemum species)
Chrysanthemums produce allelopathic compounds that can inhibit the growth of nearby plants, particularly lettuce and beans. They are often used as natural pest deterrents but can also affect certain crops.

Corn (Zea mays)
Corn releases allelopathic chemicals that can hinder the growth of tomatoes, cabbage, and broccoli.

Eucalyptus
Eucalyptus leaves contain toxic oils that leach into the soil, preventing seed germination and affecting most vegetables and herbs.

Fennel (Foeniculum vulgare)
Fennel releases chemicals that hinder germination and stunt the growth of nearby plants, particularly tomatoes, beans, cilantro, carrots, and most vegetables.

Garlic & Onions (Allium family)
Garlic and onions emit sulfur compounds that can interfere with the root development of legumes like beans, peas, and asparagus.

Mint (Mentha species)
Mint spreads aggressively and releases compounds that can suppress the growth of nearby herbs like parsley and chamomile.

Mustard (Brassica juncea)
Mustard plants release glucosinolates into the soil, which can inhibit the growth of other plants, especially legumes and some grasses.

Rye (Secale cereale)
Rye produces allelopathic chemicals that can suppress weeds and certain crops like lettuce and radishes. It's often used as a cover crop but can affect sensitive plants.

Sage (Salvia officinalis)
Sage produces natural oils that can stunt the growth of cucumbers.

Sorghum (Sorghum bicolor)
Sorghum releases sorgoleone, a compound that inhibits the growth of weeds and some crops like tomatoes and beans.

Sunflowers (Helianthus annuus)

Sunflowers produce allelopathic compounds from their roots and seed hulls, which can slow the germination and growth of beans, potatoes, and lettuce.

Walnut & Hickory Trees

These trees contain juglone, a chemical highly toxic to many garden crops, including nightshades and apples.

While managing allelopathy helps create a harmonious garden environment, another key to a thriving garden is keeping pests at bay without harming the ecosystem. Just as plants interact with each other through chemicals, they also interact with insects—both harmful and beneficial. By adopting eco-friendly pest management strategies, you can protect your plants while supporting a balanced, healthy garden. Let's explore some sustainable ways to manage pests that work in harmony with nature, ensuring your garden remains vibrant and productive.

Eco-Friendly Pest Management Strategies

Imagine a garden where plants naturally fend off pests without the need for harsh chemicals. Such a space is not only possible but more sustainable through the strategic use of companion planting. As discussed before, certain plants have innate abilities to deter pests, acting as natural defenders for their neighbors. Aromatic herbs like rosemary play a crucial role in this setup. Their strong scents confuse and repel insects, making them excellent companions for a variety of vegetables. When placed strategically throughout your garden, these herbs can create an aromatic barrier that pests find unappealing, protecting the plants you wish to thrive.

Another powerful strategy is trap cropping, where you plant a sacrificial crop specifically to attract pests away from your main crops. For example, nasturtiums can lure aphids and caterpillars away from more vulnerable plants like brassicas. By diverting pests to these trap crops, you safeguard your primary harvests. This method requires careful observation and timing but can effectively reduce pest pressures without resorting to chemical interventions. The combination of aromatic herbs and trap crops forms a dynamic duo in organic pest management, leveraging the natural properties of plants to maintain balance in the garden.

Ladybugs and lacewings are prime examples of predatory insects that feast on common garden pests such as aphids. By planting flowers like dill and cosmos you can create an inviting habitat that encourages their presence. These insects act as natural pest regulators, reducing populations of harmful bugs and promoting a healthier garden ecosystem.

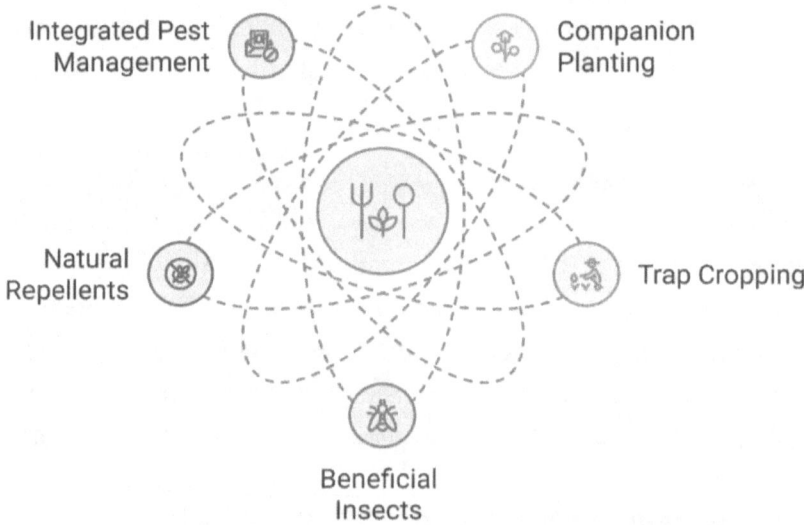

Eco-Friendly Pest Management Strategies

Another powerful technique to protect your garden from unwanted guests and keep your plants healthy is integrated pest management (IPM). Let's look at it in more detail.

Keeping Your Garden Healthy: Understanding Integrated Pest Management (IPM)

Imagine your garden is like a little community, and sometimes, unwanted guests—pests—show up. Integrated Pest Management, or IPM, is like having a smart, thoughtful neighborhood watch. It's a way to deal with pests in a balanced and safe way, without reaching for harsh chemicals.

What is IPM?

IPM is a mix of strategies to keep pests under control. It's a sustainable approach, meaning it's good for your garden, your health, and the environment. Instead of just spraying pesticides, IPM focuses on preventing pest problems in the first place and using natural methods whenever possible.

How Does IPM Work?

Here are the main ideas behind IPM:

- **Know Your Enemy** - First, you need to know what pests you're dealing with. Regular checks of your garden help you spot problems early.
- **Don't Overreact** - Don't panic at the first sign of a bug. We only take action when pests are causing real damage to our plants.
- **Prevention is Key** - Stop pests from accessing your plants. This might mean planting pest-resistant varieties, rotating crops, or using physical barriers like row covers.
- **Use Natural Helpers** - Use "good bugs" like ladybugs and lacewings, which eat pests. You can also try using traps or hand-pick pests off the plants.
- **Chemicals as a Last Resort** - If natural methods aren't enough, use pesticides, but only when absolutely necessary and in a way that minimizes harm to the environment.

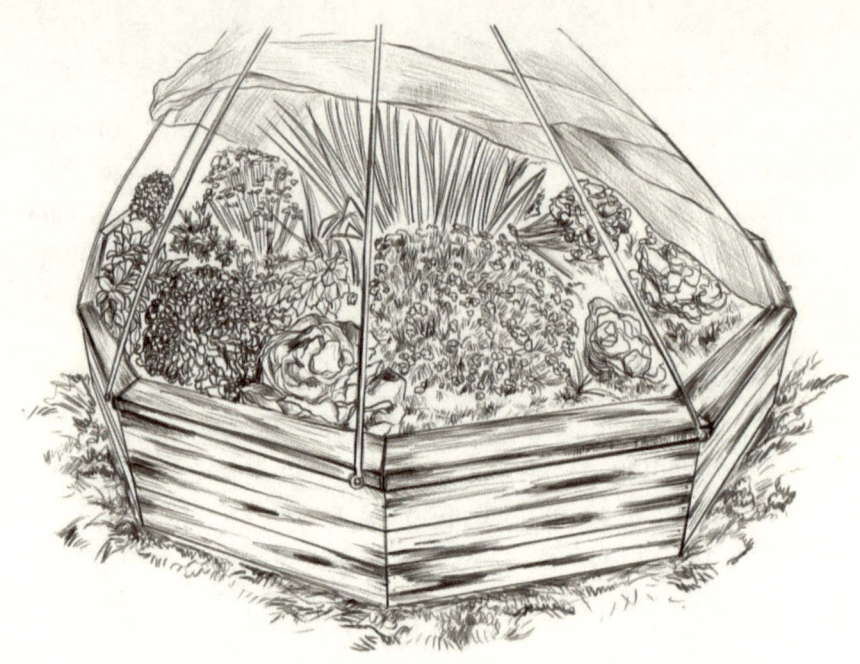

IPM Techniques in Action:

Some important forms of controls used in IPM include:

- **Cultural Controls** - Simple techniques to make your garden less inviting to pests. For example, changing when and where you plant or using mulch can help.
- **Biological Controls** - Use of natural predators to control pests. It's like having a team of superheroes fighting for your garden.
- **Chemical Controls** - Careful use of pesticides, only when needed. The goal is to choose less harmful options and apply them precisely.

Ultimately, Integrated Pest Management is a smart choice for any gardener because it embraces sustainability. By prioritizing preventative measures and natural pest control, IPM significantly reduces the need for harmful chemical pesticides, creating a healthier environment for both you and your plants. This approach not only minimizes risks but can also be more cost-effective in the long run, as it reduces reliance on expensive chemical treatments. Furthermore, IPM fosters a balanced ecosystem, encouraging biodiversity and supporting the natural predators that keep pest populations in check. In essence, IPM is a holistic strategy that benefits your garden, your wallet, and the planet.

Organic Methods of Pest Control

Organic pest control aims to control pest populations without damaging the environment. Artificial pesticides tend to leave their residue on fruits and vegetables, which may cause harm to the person consuming them. Moreover, they kill a wide range of insects, which may be beneficial for our plants. Excessive use of chemical pesticides can also drive away pollinators from your vegetable and fruit garden, causing a significant reduction in harvest.

The word "organic" refers to substances that are naturally found in the environment and contain carbon. Organic methods of pest control include a range of natural products that successfully get rid of harmful insects and pathogens, such as pyrethrum, lime, sulfur, soaps, vinegar, and salts.

You can keep your garden healthy by putting up barriers to keep the pests out and encouraging beneficial insect populations that feed on them. Strong, healthy plants are capable of defending themselves. So, providing your plants with the necessary nutrition and watering regularly goes a long way in protecting your garden.

In addition to taking better care of your plants, you can nip problems in the bud by keeping an eye out for signs of disease. Some changes in your plants that could signal trouble include leaf curling, dropping, and yellowing and the appearance of sticky honeydew on the foliage. Stunted plant growth and decreased fruiting and flowering are also signs that your plant needs help. Keep in mind that these can also be the signs of under- or overwatering, as well as of various nutrient deficiencies. A combination of symptoms is usually required for an accurate diagnosis.

Most pest problems can be avoided by using barriers such as fleece and netting to protect your plants or using sticky sheets to catch moths before they lay their larvae. However, I'm not a big fan of this method, since it can also catch beneficial insects.

Buying pest-resistant cultivars and using fresh compost can also contribute toward reducing pest problems. Copper tape placed around cloches and pots can help deter snails and slugs. The copper reacts with the slime produced by these creatures, producing mild electric shocks that stop them in their tracks

Here are some more effective strategies for getting rid of garden bugs and preventing disease:

- ***Bacillus thuringiensis (Bt)*:** Spray *Bt* solution around your plants to get rid of harmful pests. When this organic insecticide is consumed by pests, it produces proteins that paralyze their digestive system, causing them to stop feeding and die. It does not harm beneficial insects such as earthworms, nematodes, and ladybugs.
- ***Diatomaceous Earth (DE)*:** Sprinkle DE around your plants. It can penetrate the exoskeleton of several pests such as leafhoppers, cutworms, and root maggots, causing dehydration and killing them off.
- ***Discard affected plant parts***: Cut and dispose of affected plant parts to limit spread of disease.
- ***Handpicking*:** Pick insects that are visible to the eye like cutworms, and beetles, cabbage loopers and drop them into soapy water to kill them.
- ***Netting:*** It is an effective solution for keeping out large predators. You can support it with canes and weigh it down at the base so that it doesn't get blown away by strong winds.
- ***Neem oil*:** Mix two teaspoons of neem oil and one teaspoon liquid soap dissolved in one quart of water and spray on your plants to eliminate aphids, leafhoppers, whiteflies, and scale insects.

- **Soap and water mixture**: Mix one teaspoon of dish soap or soap dissolved in one quart of water and spray on the plant to get rid of spider mites, aphids, thrips, and whiteflies. You can also add vegetable oil to this mixture. The oil coats the bodies of the aforementioned insects, suffocating them.
- *Vinegar mixture:* you can easily create your own insecticidal soap from a gallon (3-7 liter) water, 2 tbs white vinegar, 2 tbs dish detergent, and 2 tbs baking soda. Spray this mixture under the leaves of the plants where white fly eggs, scale and adults reside.
- **Water:** Hose down the plants with a blast of water to knock off pests like aphids, spider mites, and whiteflies.

Integrating Pollinator-Friendly Practices

As you walk through a garden buzzing with life, the role of pollinators becomes immediately clear. Bees, butterflies, and birds are vital contributors to the garden ecosystem. They move from bloom to bloom, transferring pollen and enabling plants to set fruit and seeds. Without these industrious creatures, many of the fruits and vegetables we enjoy would struggle to develop.

Year-round flowering plants play a crucial role in maintaining this biodiversity. By selecting a variety of plants that bloom at different times, you ensure that your garden always has something to offer its pollinators. Early spring flowers provide much-needed resources after winter, while late-bloomers extend the feeding season into fall. This continuous cycle of flowering not only supports pollinators but keeps your garden visually interesting throughout the year.

To attract these pollinators, consider planting a variety of blooms that provide both nectar and pollen. Lavender, with its fragrant purple flowers, draws bees and butterflies while adding a touch of elegance to any garden. Sunflowers, towering and bright, not only offer a feast for pollinators but bring cheer to your space. These plants, along with others like coneflowers and bee balm, create a welcoming environment for pollinators, ensuring they have what they need to thrive. The diversity of plants offers continuous blooms throughout the growing season, providing a consistent food source for these vital creatures.

Creating a pollinator-friendly habitat involves more than just planting the right flowers. Providing water sources and nesting sites can make your garden even more inviting. A shallow dish filled with water and pebbles serves as a simple pollinator bath, offering refreshment on hot days. Consider leaving small patches of bare soil or a pile of twigs in a sunny corner for ground-nesting bees. These thoughtful additions transform your garden into a sanctuary where pollinators can live and work efficiently. Consider building a bug house in your garden. You can also find a wide selection of hummingbird and butterfly feeders online throughout the year. Such spaces not only attract pollinators but support their lifecycle, encouraging them to return year after year.

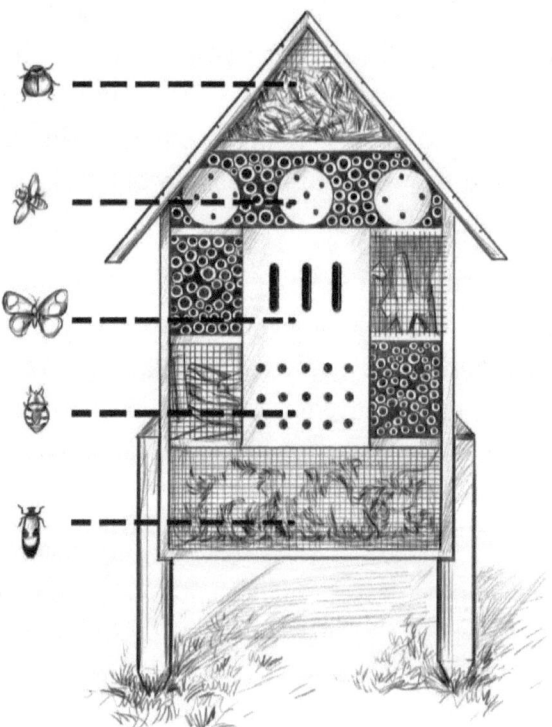

Figure 5.1: Bug hotel.

The benefits of biodiversity in your garden extend beyond attracting pollinators. A diverse range of plants supports a broader ecosystem, inviting not just pollinators but beneficial insects such as ladybugs and hoverflies. These insects help control pest populations naturally, reducing the need for chemical interventions. Moreover, a garden rich in biodiversity is more resilient to pests and diseases, as the variety of plants and insects creates a balanced environment that can withstand and recover from disturbances more quickly.

Adapting Your Garden for Seasonal Changes

Each season offers unique opportunities and challenges for planting. Cool-season crops such as lettuce, peas, and broccoli thrive in the brisk temperatures of spring and fall, while warm-season crops like tomatoes, peppers, and cucumbers flourish under the summer sun. Timing is everything; planting cool-season crops too late may result in bolting, where plants prematurely flower and go to seed. Conversely, warm-season crops sown too early might succumb to late frosts.

Adapting your garden's infrastructure to accommodate seasonal changes is equally important. As temperatures drop, consider using row covers or greenhouses to protect tender plants from frost and extend your growing season. Row covers, made from lightweight fabric, act as a barrier against cold, while greenhouses provide a controlled environment where you can regulate temperature and humidity. These structures allow you to grow a wider variety of plants, even in challenging climates, by creating microclimates that support plant health and growth. Additionally, they can help manage pests by providing a physical barrier that keeps unwanted visitors at bay.

To better understand these concepts, imagine a garden layout designed to transition seamlessly from spring to fall. In spring, your garden might feature neat rows of cool-season crops like spinach and radishes, thriving in the mild temperatures. As summer approaches, you might replace these with heat-loving plants such as tomatoes and zucchini, taking advantage of the longer days and increased warmth.

By fall, the garden could transition back to hardy greens and root vegetables, making use of the cooler weather.

Preparing your garden for winter is not just about surviving the cold months; it's about setting the stage for continuous growth and productivity. By giving your soil the attention it deserves, you ensure that it retains its vitality, ready to nurture your plants when the days grow long again.

Conclusion

As we come to the end of our journey through the world of companion planting, I want to briefly reflect on the purpose of this book. My goal has been to empower you with practical, chemical-free techniques that will help you create a thriving, resilient garden all year round. By understanding the basics of companion planting, mastering plant pairings, designing efficient garden spaces, and implementing sustainable practices, you can achieve a garden that is not only productive but in harmony with nature.

Throughout this book, we've covered a wealth of information to support your gardening journey. We've explored the science behind plant synergy, the benefits of companion planting for soil health, and the importance of biodiversity in your garden. You've learned how to create a perennial and annual mix, utilize herbs for companion benefits, and integrate pollinator-friendly practices.

As you reflect on these concepts, I hope you feel empowered to apply these methods in your own garden. It's important to remember that gardening is a journey of continuous learning and adaptation. There may be challenges along the way, but with the right knowledge and tools, you can overcome them. Don't be afraid to experiment, make mistakes, and learn from your experiences. Every season brings new opportunities to refine your skills and deepen your connection with the earth.

Remember, you're not alone in this endeavor. The gardening community is robust and thriving. Connect with other gardeners in your area, join online forums, or participate in community gardening initiatives.

On a personal note, I want to express my gratitude to you for choosing this guide. It's been a joy to share my passion for gardening with you, and I hope that the information and inspiration within these pages will support your own gardening endeavors. As you continue on this path, remember that every seed you plant, every soil you nurture, and every harvest you reap is a testament to your dedication and love for the earth.

So, my fellow gardeners, let us go forth with curiosity, compassion, and a deep respect for the natural world. May your gardens be filled with abundance, your harvests bountiful, and your hearts full of the joy that only comes from nurturing life from seed to table. Happy gardening!

Quick guide for beginner's favorites

Plant	Good companions	Bad companions
Asparagus	Basil, Marigold, Parsley, Dill, Tomato, Nasturtium	Garlic, Potato, Onions
Beans	Potato, Marigold, Cucumbers, Squash, Summer Savory, Corn	Tomato, Pepper, Chives, Garlic, Onions
Beets	Mint, Garlic, Onions, Leeks, Scallon, Broccoli, Cauliflower, Brussels sprouts, Radish, Kale, Cabbage	Pole beans
Broccoli	Dill, Mint, Rosemary	Strawberry, Mustard, Tomato, Oregano
Cabbage	Onions, Dill, Oregano, Sage, Mint, Chamomille, Nasturtium, Clover, Beets	Strawberry, Tomato, Peppers, Eggplant
Corn	Cucumber, Beans, Melons, Parsley, Squash, Marigold, Pumpkin	Tomato
Cucumber	Radish, Lettuce, Onions, Dill, Nasturtium, Corn, Beans	Potato, Sage
Eggplant	Catnip, Spinach, Peppers, Nasturtium, Marigold, Sunflower, Bush beans, Thyme, Tarragon, Tomato, Potato	Fennel
Lettuce	Radish, Dill, Cucumber, Carrot, Strawberry	Beans, Beets, Cabbage, Parsley
Peppers	Beans, Tomato, Onions, Geranium, Petunia	Fennel
Potato	Eggplant, Beans, Cabbage, Peas, Sage, Corn, Nasturtium, Catnip, Coriander	Cucumber, Tomato, Pumpkin, Spinach, Fennel, Onions, Squash, Fennel, Raspberries
Pumpkin	Melons, Corn, Dill, Radish, Beans, Oregano	Potato
Spinach	Cauliflower, Strawberry, Radish, Eggplant	Potato
Squash	Onion, Corn, Mint, Nasturtium, Dill, Peas, Beans, Radish	Potato
Tomato	Carrot, Parsley, Basil, Marigold, Garlic, Asparagus, Collards	Corn, Cabbage, Broccoli, Brussels sprouts, Potato
Turnip	Radish, Cauliflower, Beans, Lettuce, Spinach, Broccoli, Cabbage, Peas, Tomato, Brussels sprouts, Mint	Carrot, Parsley and other root crops
Zucchini	Nasturtium, Corn, Beans	Potato

Companion Plants for Vegetables 1.

Vegetable	Good Companions	Bad Companions	Notes
Asparagus	Tomatoes	Garlic, onions, potatoes	Tomatoes repel asparagus beetles; avoid planting near alliums or potatoes.
Beans (Bush)	Carrots, cucumbers, corn, celery, potatoes	Garlic, onions, shallots	Beans fix nitrogen in the soil; avoid planting near alliums.
Beans (Pole)	Corn, radishes, spinach	Beets, garlic, onions, shallots	Corn provides a natural trellis; avoid planting near alliums.
Beets	Broccoli, Brussels sprouts, cabbage, cauliflower, lettuce, onions	Pole beans	Beets grow well with brassicas; avoid planting near pole beans.
Broccoli	Beets, celery, onions, potatoes	Strawberries, tomatoes, pole beans	Avoid planting near strawberries or tomatoes to prevent competition.
Brussels Sprouts	Beets, celery, onions, potatoes	Strawberries, tomatoes	Similar to broccoli and cabbage; avoid planting near strawberries or tomatoes.
Cabbage	Beets, celery, onions, potatoes	Strawberries, tomatoes, pole beans	Avoid planting near strawberries or tomatoes to prevent competition.
Carrots	Beans, leeks, lettuce, onions, peas, tomatoes	Dill, parsnips, potatoes	Onions and leeks repel carrot flies; avoid planting near dill or potatoes.
Cauliflower	Beets, celery, onions, potatoes	Strawberries, tomatoes, pole beans	Similar to broccoli and cabbage; avoid planting near strawberries or tomatoes.
Celery	Beans, cabbage, cauliflower, leeks, onions, tomatoes	Corn, potatoes	Celery benefits from the shade of taller plants; avoid planting near corn or potatoes.
Corn	Beans, cucumbers, peas, potatoes, pumpkins, squash	Tomatoes	Corn provides support for climbing plants; avoid planting near tomatoes.
Cucumbers	Beans, corn, peas, radishes	Potatoes	Radishes deter cucumber beetles; avoid planting near potatoes.
Eggplant	Beans, spinach	None	Eggplant benefits from nitrogen-fixing beans.
Garlic	Beets, carrots, cucumbers, lettuce, tomatoes	Beans, peas, asparagus	Garlic repels pests; avoid planting near legumes.
Kale	Beets, celery, cucumbers, onions, spinach	Strawberries, tomatoes	Avoid planting near strawberries or tomatoes to prevent competition.

Companion Plants for Vegetables 2.

Vegetable	Good Companions	Bad Companions	Notes
Leeks	Carrots, celery, onions, strawberries	Beans, peas	Leeks repel carrot flies; avoid planting near legumes.
Lettuce	Beets, carrots, cucumbers, onions, radishes, strawberries, tomatoes	Cabbage, celery	Lettuce benefits from shade provided by taller plants like tomatoes.
Okra	Beans, cucumbers, peppers	None	Okra grows well with beans and cucumbers.
Onions	Beets, carrots, lettuce, tomatoes	Beans, peas, asparagus	Onions repel pests; avoid planting near legumes.
Parsnips	Beans, carrots, onions, peas	None	Parsnips grow well with nitrogen-fixing plants like beans and peas.
Peas	Carrots, corn, cucumbers, radishes, turnips, beans	Garlic, onions, shallots, potatoes	Peas fix nitrogen in the soil; avoid planting near alliums or potatoes.
Peppers	Carrots, onions, spinach, tomatoes	Beans, brassicas	Avoid planting near beans or brassicas to prevent stunted growth.
Potatoes	Beans, corn, cabbage, eggplant, peas	Cucumbers, pumpkins, squash, tomatoes	Avoid planting near tomatoes or cucumbers to prevent disease spread.
Pumpkins	Corn, beans	Potatoes	Corn provides shade; avoid planting near potatoes.
Radishes	Beans, carrots, cucumbers, lettuce, peas, spinach	Cabbage, cauliflower, broccoli	Radishes deter pests like cucumber beetles; avoid planting near brassicas.
Rutabagas	Peas, beans	Potatoes	Rutabagas grow well with nitrogen-fixing plants; avoid planting near potatoes.
Spinach	Cabbage, cauliflower, celery, eggplant, onions, peas	Potatoes	Spinach grows well with nitrogen-fixing plants like peas.
Sweet Potatoes	Beans	None	Sweet potatoes benefit from nitrogen-fixing beans.
Tomatoes	Carrots, celery, onions, lettuce, spinach	Brassicas (e.g., broccoli, cabbage), corn, potatoes	Avoid planting near brassicas or potatoes to prevent competition and disease spread.
Turnips	Peas, beans	Potatoes	Turnips grow well with nitrogen-fixing plants; avoid planting near potatoes.
Zucchini/Squash	Beans, corn, radishes	Potatoes	Avoid planting near potatoes to prevent competition.

Companion Plants for Fruits 1.

Fruit	Good Companions	Bad Companions
Apple	Chives, Garlic, Clover, Dill, Yarrow, Nasturtiums, Comfrey, Borage, Chamomile, Mint, Tansy, Lavender, Rosemary, Thyme, Sage, Marigolds, Carrots, Beets, Spinach, Peas, Beans, Lettuce	Potatoes, Tomatoes, Cabbage family (potential disease and nutrient competition), Fennel, Black Walnut
Apricot	Chives, Garlic, Clover, Dill, Yarrow, Nasturtiums, Comfrey, Borage, Chamomile, Mint, Tansy, Lavender, Rosemary, Thyme, Sage, Marigolds, Carrots, Beets, Spinach, Peas, Beans, Lettuce	Potatoes, Tomatoes, Cabbage family (potential disease and nutrient competition), Fennel, Black Walnut
Blackcurrant	Garlic, Chives, Marigolds, Nasturtiums, Chamomile, Borage, Comfrey, Lavender, Rosemary, Thyme, Sage, Carrots, Beets, Spinach, Lettuce, Peas, Beans	Fennel, Black Walnut, Cabbage Family (some competition)
Blueberry	Phacelia, Buckwheat, Clover, Lupine, Mint, Azaleas, Rhododendrons, Pine Trees, Oak Trees, Strawberries, Cranberries, Huckleberries, Legumes (Beans, Peas), Mustard Greens, Radishes, Carrots, Beets, Lettuce, Spinach, Dill, Chamomile, Yarrow,	Cabbage family (heavy feeders that can compete for nutrients, also blueberries like acidic soil so cabbage might influence them), Tomatoes, Potatoes, Peppers, Eggplant, Cucumbers, Melons
Boysenberry	Marigolds, Nasturtiums, Garlic, Chives, Dill, Chamomile, Thyme, Borage, Lavender, Parsley, Rosemary, Sage, Mint, Tansy, Comfrey, Clover, Yarrow, Potatoes, Asparagus, Rhubarb, Lettuce, Spinach, Carrots, Beets, Peas, Beans	Potatoes, Tomatoes, Peppers, Eggplant, Cucumbers, Melons, Squash, Fennel, Black Walnut, Cabbage family
Cherry	Chives, Garlic, Clover, Dill, Yarrow, Nasturtiums, Comfrey, Borage, Chamomile, Mint, Tansy, Lavender, Rosemary, Thyme, Sage, Marigolds, Carrots, Beets, Spinach, Peas, Beans, Lettuce	Potatoes, Tomatoes, Cabbage family (potential disease and nutrient competition), Fennel, Black Walnut
Cranberry	Blueberries, Huckleberries, Strawberries, Heather, Pine Trees, Oak Trees, Azaleas, Rhododendrons, Clover, Lupine, Legumes (Beans, Peas), Mustard Greens, Radishes, Carrots, Beets, Lettuce, Spinach, Dill, Chamomile, Yarrow, Mint	Cabbage family (heavy feeders that can compete for nutrients, also cranberries like acidic soil so cabbage might influence them), Tomatoes, Potatoes, Peppers, Eggplant, Cucumbers, Melons
Grapes	Basil, Oregano, Marigolds, Lavender, Clover, Rosemary, Sage, Thyme, Chamomile, Dill, Yarrow, Nasturtiums, Carrots, Beets, Lettuce, Spinach, Peas, Beans	Cabbage, Broccoli, Brussel Sprouts, Fennel, Black Walnut, Potatoes, Tomatoes
Gooseberry	Garlic, Chives, Marigolds, Nasturtiums, Chamomile, Borage, Comfrey, Lavender, Rosemary, Thyme, Sage, Carrots, Beets, Spinach, Lettuce, Peas, Beans	Fennel, Black Walnut, Cabbage Family (some competition)

Companion Plants for Fruits 2.

Fruit	Good Companions	Bad Companions
Honeyberry	Strawberries, Clover, Lupine, Azaleas, Rhododendrons, Legumes (Beans, Peas), Mustard Greens, Radishes, Carrots, Beets, Lettuce, Spinach, Dill, Chamomile, Yarrow, Mint	Cabbage family (can compete for nutrients), Tomatoes, Potatoes, Peppers, Eggplant, Cucumbers, Melons
Jostaberry	Garlic, Chives, Marigolds, Nasturtiums, Chamomile, Borage, Comfrey, Lavender, Rosemary, Thyme, Sage, Carrots, Beets, Spinach, Lettuce, Peas, Beans	Fennel, Black Walnut, Cabbage Family (some competition)
Kiwi	Nasturtiums, Comfrey, Borage, Lavender, Chamomile, Mint, Tansy, Marigolds, Carrots, Beets, Spinach, Peas, Beans, Lettuce, Rosemary, Sage, Thyme, Chives, Garlic, Clover, Dill, Yarrow	Potatoes, Tomatoes, Cabbage family (potential disease and nutrient competition), Fennel, Black Walnut
Loganberry	Marigolds, Nasturtiums, Garlic, Chives, Dill, Chamomile, Thyme, Borage, Lavender, Parsley, Rosemary, Sage, Mint, Tansy, Comfrey, Clover, Yarrow, Potatoes, Asparagus, Rhubarb, Lettuce, Spinach, Carrots, Beets, Peas, Beans	Potatoes, Tomatoes, Peppers, Eggplant, Cucumbers, Melons, Squash, Fennel, Black Walnut, Cabbage family
Pear	Chives, Garlic, Clover, Dill, Yarrow, Nasturtiums, Comfrey, Borage, Chamomile, Mint, Tansy, Lavender, Rosemary, Thyme, Sage, Marigolds, Carrots, Beets, Spinach, Peas, Beans, Lettuce	Potatoes, Tomatoes, Cabbage family (potential disease and nutrient competition), Fennel, Black Walnut
Physalis (Cape Gooseberry)	Borage, Thyme, Marigolds, Nasturtiums, Basil, Oregano, Rosemary, Sage, Carrots, Beets, Lettuce, Spinach, Peas, Beans	Potatoes, Tomatoes, Peppers, Eggplant, Cucumbers, Melons, Squash, Fennel, Black Walnut, Cabbage family
Plum	Chives, Garlic, Clover, Dill, Yarrow, Nasturtiums, Comfrey, Borage, Chamomile, Mint, Tansy, Lavender, Rosemary, Thyme, Sage, Marigolds, Carrots, Beets, Spinach, Peas, Beans, Lettuce	Potatoes, Tomatoes, Cabbage family (potential disease and nutrient competition), Fennel, Black Walnut
Quince	Chives, Garlic, Clover, Dill, Yarrow, Nasturtiums, Comfrey, Borage, Chamomile, Mint, Tansy, Lavender, Rosemary, Thyme, Sage, Marigolds, Carrots, Beets, Spinach, Peas, Beans, Lettuce	Potatoes, Tomatoes, Cabbage family (potential disease and nutrient competition), Fennel, Black Walnut
Raspberry	Marigolds, Nasturtiums, Garlic, Chives, Dill, Chamomile, Thyme, Borage, Lavender, Parsley, Rosemary, Sage, Mint, Tansy, Comfrey, Clover, Yarrow, Potatoes, Asparagus, Rhubarb, Lettuce, Spinach, Carrots, Beets, Peas, Beans	Potatoes, Tomatoes, Peppers, Eggplant, Cucumbers, Melons, Squash, Fennel, Black Walnut, Cabbage family

Companion Plants for Fruits 3.

Fruit	Good Companions	Bad Companions
Redcurrant	Garlic, Chives, Marigolds, Nasturtiums, Chamomile, Borage, Comfrey, Lavender, Rosemary, Thyme, Sage, Carrots, Beets, Spinach, Lettuce, Peas, Beans	Fennel, Black Walnut, Cabbage Family (some competition)
Strawberry	Borage, Thyme, Bush Beans, Lettuce, Spinach, Garlic, Onions, Dill, Chamomile, Carrots, Parsley, Marigolds, Rosemary, Sage, Lavender, Chives, Beets, Radishes	Cabbage family (can attract pests that also affect strawberries), Potatoes, Tomatoes, Peppers, Eggplant, Cucumbers, Melons, Squash
Tayberry	Marigolds, Nasturtiums, Garlic, Chives, Dill, Chamomile, Thyme, Borage, Lavender, Parsley, Rosemary, Sage, Mint, Tansy, Comfrey, Clover, Yarrow, Potatoes, Asparagus, Rhubarb, Lettuce, Spinach, Carrots, Beets, Peas, Beans	Potatoes, Tomatoes, Peppers, Eggplant, Cucumbers, Melons, Squash, Fennel, Black Walnut, Cabbage family
Thornless Blackberry	Marigolds, Nasturtiums, Garlic, Chives, Dill, Chamomile, Thyme, Borage, Lavender, Parsley, Rosemary, Sage, Mint, Tansy, Comfrey, Clover, Yarrow, Potatoes, Asparagus, Rhubarb, Lettuce, Spinach, Carrots, Beets, Peas, Beans	Potatoes, Tomatoes, Peppers, Eggplant, Cucumbers, Melons, Squash, Fennel, Black Walnut, Cabbage family
Wintergreen	Blueberries, Cranberries, Huckleberries, Strawberries, Heather, Pine Trees, Oak Trees, Azaleas, Rhododendrons, Clover, Lupine, Legumes (Beans, Peas), Mustard Greens, Radishes, Carrots, Beets, Lettuce, Spinach, Dill, Chamomile, Yarrow, Mint	Cabbage family (heavy feeders that can compete for nutrients, also wintergreen like acidic soil so cabbage might influence them), Tomatoes, Potatoes, Peppers, Eggplant, Cucumbers, Melons

Companion Plants for Herbs 1.

Herb	Annual or Perennial?	Good Companions	Bad Companions
Anise	Annual	Cabbage, Coriander.	Basil, Rosemary, Thyme
Arugula/Rocket	Annual	Carrots, Radishes, Garlic.	Thyme
Basil	Annual, Perennial in Zones 10+	Tomatoes, Peppers, Asparagus, Oregano, Cabbage, Rosemary, Marigolds.	Rue
Bay Laurel	Perennial	Rosemary, Sage, Thyme.	
Borage	Annual	Strawberries, Tomatoes, Squash, Cabbage, Marigolds.	
Calendula	Annual	Tomatoes, Cabbage, Rosemary, Thyme.	
Chamomile	Annual	Cabbage, Onions, Broccoli, Kale, Basil, Rosemary.	
Chervil	Annual	Lettuce, Radishes.	
Chives	Perennial	Carrots, Tomatoes, Strawberries, Roses, Fruit Trees, Lettuce, Beets, Cabbage, Garlic, Marigolds	Beans, Peas
Cilantro/Coriander	Annual	Carrots, Potatoes, Spinach, Dill.	Fennel
Dill	Annual	Cabbage, Cucumbers, Lettuce, Onions.	Carrots, Tomatoes
Flax	Annual	Carrots, Potatoes.	
Garlic Chives	Perennial	Carrots, Tomatoes, Strawberries, Roses, Fruit Trees, Lettuce, Beets, Cabbage, Garlic, Marigolds	Beans, Peas
Lavender	Perennial	Cabbage, Rosemary, Thyme, Garlic, Beets, Carrots, Kale, Marigolds, Chamomile, Oregano, Basil	Fennel, Mint (can be invasive and compete), Rue
Lemon Balm	Perennial	Tomatoes, Cabbage, Broccoli.	
Lemon Verbena	Perennial	Rosemary, Sage, Thyme.	
Lovage	Perennial	Beans, Peas, Potatoes, Tomatoes, Lettuce, Rosemary, Sage, Borage	Fennel

Companion Plants for Herbs 2.

Herb	Annual or Perennial?	Good Companions	Bad Companions
Marjoram	Perennial	Beans, Cabbage, Rosemary, Thyme, Oregano	Cucumbers
Mint	Perennial	Cabbage, Tomatoes, Broccoli, Kale, Carrots, Beets, Lavender, Thyme, Rosemary	Cucumbers, Parsley, Dill
Mustard	Annual	Beans, Peas.	
Nasturtium	Annual	Cabbage, Tomatoes, Cucumbers, Fruit Trees.	
Oregano	Perennial	Beans, Cabbage, Rosemary, Thyme, Lavender, Basil, Tomatoes, Peppers	Cucumbers, Fennel
Rosemary	Perennial	Cabbage, Carrots, Beans, Sage, Thyme, Lavender, Marigolds, Borage, Nasturtiums, Garlic, Chives	Cucumbers (some sources say cucumbers do well, but some do not, monitor), Kohlrabi, Sage, Thyme, Parsley, Fennel
Rue	Perennial	Roses, Lavender	Basil, Sage, Mint
Sage	Perennial	Rosemary, Cabbage, Carrots, Strawberries, Lavender, Thyme	Cucumbers, Fennel
Salad Burnet	Perennial	Cabbage, Rosemary, Thyme, Borage.	
Summer Savory	Annual	Beans, Cabbage, Rosemary, Thyme.	
Sweet Cicely	Perennial	Rosemary, Sage, Thyme, Lovage.	
Tarragon	Perennial	Cabbage, Tomatoes, Peppers, Eggplant, Rosemary, Thyme, Borage.	
Thyme	Perennial	Cabbage, Strawberries, Tomatoes, Potatoes, Rosemary, Lavender, Garlic, Beets, Marigolds, Nasturtiums, Oregano, Basil	Cucumber, Arugula, Fennel
Winter Savory	Perennial	Beans, Cabbage, Rosemary, Thyme, Oregano, Garlic	Cucumbers

Companion Plants for Flowers

Flower	Good Companions	Benefits
Alyssum	Grapes, lettuce	Attracts beneficial pollinators
Borage	Almost everything, especially beans, strawberry, cucumber, squash, fruit trees, tomatoes, and cabbage	Adds trace minerals to the soil and helps improve soil structure with its deep roots.
Calendula	Nearly all plants, particularly peppers, tomatoes, cucumbers, squash, potatoes, roses, alliums, brassicas, and zucchini	Attracts beneficial insects and can attract some of the pests that might otherwise attack leafy vegetables
Chamomile	Cabbages and other brassicas, cucumbers, onions	Attracts beneficial insects and can attract some of the pests that might otherwise attack leafy vegetables
Chrysanthemum	Generally compatible with most plants, but can inhibit the growth of lettuce due to their allelopathic properties.	Contains pyrethrum, a natural insect repellent effective against ants and beetles
Geraniums	Roses, corn, peppers, and grapes	Deters mosquitoes, cabbageworms, leafhoppers, japanese beetles, aphids and spider mites
Lavender	Generally compatible with most plants.	Deters mosquitoes, fleas, and moths, protecting nearby plants from these pests
Lupin	Brassica, lettuces, rosemary, dill, strawberry, rose	Improves soil and attracts beneficial insects
Marigold	Nearly all plants, particularly peppers, tomatoes, cucumbers, squash, potatoes, roses, alliums, brassicas, and zucchini	Suppresses nematodes and helps keep soil-borne pests in check, improving soil health. Deters nematodes and aphids
Nasturtium	Beans, squash, tomatoes, fruit trees, brassicas, radish, cucumbers	Deters nematodes and aphids
	Their sprawling nature can overshadow smaller plants.	Nasturtiums can attract pests (aphids, whiteflies, cabbage worms, squash bugs, flea beetles) that may also affect beans and brassicas and attack leafy vegetables. (trap cropping)
Pansy	Alliums, onions, roses	
Petunia	Squash, pumpkins, cucumbers, asparagus	
Rose	Chives, garlic, marigold	garlic deters pests and prevents diseases
Sunflower	Peppers, corn, soybeans, tomatoes, swan plant	Attracts pollinators and beneficial insects, but may compete for resources and attract pests harmful to cucumbers..
Tansy	Beans, brassicas, cucumbers, squash, raspberries and other berries, roses, corn, fruit trees	Repels certain pests, but can inhibit the growth of collard greens due to its allelopathic properties.

Sun Map

Zone	Time				

Thanks for Reading, Please Leave a Review!

I would be *incredibly appreciative* if you could rate my book or leave a review on **Amazon**.

Just scan this QR code with your phone, or visit the
https://Companion.SophieMckay.com
link to land directly on
the book's Amazon review page.

Your review not only helps me create better books, but also helps more fellow gardener experience success in the garden and put healthy food on their family's table.

Thank you!

Before we begin, go and grab your FREE gifts!

Sophie McKay's Seed Starting & Planting Calculator
+ The Ultimate Guide to Organic Weed Management

In these free resources, you will discover:

- The perfect Seed Starting and Planting times for YOUR region or zone
- The 8 Organic Weed Removal Methods
- The 6 best and proven Weed Management Methods
- The tools you did NOT know you need for a weed-free garden
- How weeds can help your yard
- How to identify which weed is good and which is bad for a yard or garden
- The difference between Invasive and Noxious Weeds

Get your FREE copy today by visiting:
https://sophiemckay.com/free-resources/

Unlock the Secrets to Thriving Fruit Tree Gardens!

Transform your backyard orchard dreams into reality with 'Beginner's Guide to Growing Fruit Trees Fast and Easy.' Your guide on this road will be Sophie McKay, an avid gardener and an emerging author in gardening, permaculture, and sustainability. She'll share her best tips and tricks to ensure your gardening journey succeeds.

From **efficient** garden **layout design to selecting healthy trees, introducing pruning and grafting basics, mastering sustainable pest management, and creating a permaculture-inspired food forest**—this guide is your go-to resource for cultivating a vibrant and fruitful orchard. With practical insights, rejuvenating techniques, and seasonal care tips, embark on a sustainable gardening success story.

Just **scan this QR code** with your phone, or visit the https://BuyFTG.SophieMckay.com link to land directly book's Amazon page.

If You Liked This Book, Try This One Too!

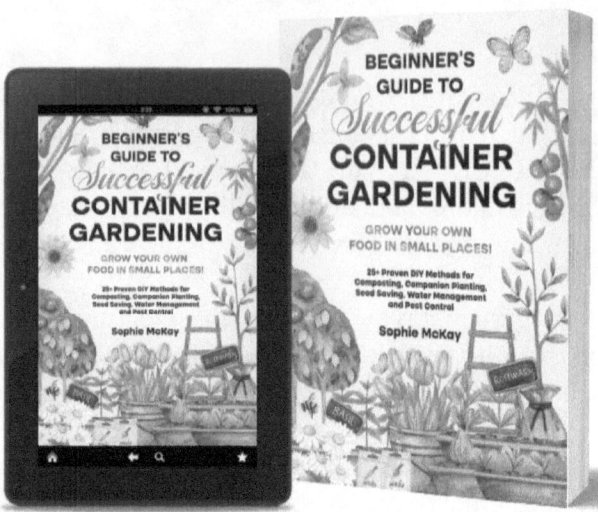

Sophie's fantastic new book, **The Beginner's Guide to Successful Container Gardening**, is now published!

Inside, **you will learn about the basics of container gardening**, including **selecting the right container, soil, and plants** for all your needs. You will also learn about the specific requirements of different types of plants, and how to care for them throughout the growing season. **Whether you're a seasoned gardener or just getting started, this book has something for everyone.**

So if you're ready for some more inspiration, check out this book now to keep your garden thriving all year round with **25+ proven DIY methods for composting, companion planting, seed saving, water management and pest control!**

So what are you waiting for? Grab it for yourself!

Just **scan this QR code** with your phone, or visit the https://Container.SophieMckay.com link to land directly on the book's Amazon page.

Welcome to Permaculture!

Unlock the secrets of a resilient garden! Discover permaculture design and **learn how to grow your own food in harmony with nature**.

Join Sophie on a guided tour and create your own **sustainable permaculture garden** with confidence. Success guaranteed!

Just scan this QR code with your phone, or visit the https://book.SophieMckay.com link to land directly on the book's Amazon page.

Bibliography

Albert, S. (n.d.). Hardy, half-hardy, and tender vegetable crops. Harvest to Table. https://url.us.m.mimecastprotect.com/s/5EPmCOYRnMip6YM0nHEfxcG2wSd?domain=harvesttotable.com/

Bordessa, K. (2021, July 16). Container vegetable gardening for beginners. Attainable Sustainable.

Can you start composting in urban areas? (2019, June 24). Greenhouse Emporium. https://url.us.m.mimecastprotect.com/s/nZGMCW6RyLc5A3VPOCpu8convoz?domain=greenhouseemporium.com/

Chase, A. (n.d.). 10 ways to keep your garden healthy. Fine Gardening. Retrieved September 12, 2022,

Container gardening secrets: Ideas to inspiration. (n.d.). Eartheasy Guides & Articles. Retrieved July 26, 2022.

Container garden maintenance tips: Help your plants thrive all summer long. (n.d.). Savvy Gardening. https://url.us.m.mimecastprotect.com/s/ncHQC1wDlWtM7glk3tAI0cVHqoG?domain=savvygardening.com/

Daron. (2020, March 24). Nitrogen fixers: What they are and tips to get started. Growing with Nature. https://url.us.m.mimecastprotect.com/s/r1UdC2kEmxSpNrgR1HpSnc5EuR0?domain=growingwithnature.org/

The Earth Box. (n.d.). How to grow a self-sufficient garden. https://url.us.m.mimecastprotect.com/s/jrDLC4xJoQsBpPqmgcoUyc4gtme?domain=earthbox.com

Engels, J. (2016, November 18). How and why to rotate your annual crops. Permaculture Research Institute. https://url.us.m.mimecastprotect.com/s/Ol6bC73kr1CAOMwQlfQhvco2GlK?domain=permaculturenews.org/

Gardening Know How. (n.d.). Finding microclimates in gardens: How to determine your microclimate. https://www.gardeningknowhow.com/garden-how-to/info/finding-microclimates-in-gardens.htm

Farmers' Almanac. (n.d.). Companion planting guide. https://www.farmersalmanac.com/companion-planting-guide

Fine Gardening. (n.d.). The benefits of raised garden beds.

Hassani, N. (2021, November 29). Companion planting with companion planting chart. The Spruce.

Huffstetler, E. (2022, July 5). How to make your own fertilizer. The Spruce.

Judd, A. S. (n.d.-b). Best way to water raised-bed gardens. Growing In The Garden. https://url.us.m.mimecastprotect.com/s/Mvx5Co2PrVTr79QBEhgTncpiCvx?domain=growinginthegarden.com/

Kanuckel, A. (2022, June 20). Companion planting guide: Sow easy. Farmers' Almanac. https://www.farmersalmanac.com/companion-planting-guide

Kellogg Garden Organics. (n.d.). Creating a pollinator friendly garden. https://url.us.m.mimecastprotect.com/s/W1mHCqx907s8pBVzZuycMcEdDXU?domain=kellogggarden.com/

Kime, L. (2012, August 28). Soil quality information. Penn State Extension. https://url.us.m.mimecastprotect.com/s/uGDvCrk6x8S85MW1EuofBc4l7VW?domain=extension.psu.edu

Know your growing zone: Cold hardiness and heat tolerance. (2013, November 15). Longfield Gardens. https://url.us.m.mimecastprotect.com/s/KJMWCv2kBlT7D1R2xUOhncQ9a6n?domain=longfield-gardens.com

Lopez, C. (n.d.). Different types of soil for gardening. Trinjal. https://url.us.m.mimecastprotect.com/s/VOHOCwplDVTGD62AKSOi7cJ9swi?domain=trinjal.com/

Magyar, C. (2020, January 14). Annuals, biennials and perennials: 3 plant types you need to know. Rural Sprout.

Markham, D. (n.d.). 8 natural & homemade insecticides: Save your garden without killing the Earth. Treehugger. https://url.us.m.mimecastprotect.com/s/mWd4CADxGNINv08n4fxCzcGNkfV?domain=treehugger.com

McKay, S. (2022). The practical permaculture project. SmartMind Publishing.

McKay, S. (2023). The Beginners Guide to Container Gardening. SmartMind Publishing.

McKay, S. (2024). The Complete Guide to Raised Bed Gardening. SmartMind Publishing.

McKay, S. (2024). The Beginner's Guide to Growing Fruit Trees Fast and Easy . SmartMind Publishing.

Michaels, K. (2022a). Vegetable container gardening for beginners. The Spruce.

Patterson, S. (n.d.). Which soil is best for plant growth? LoveToKnow Garden. https://url.us.m.mimecastprotect.com/s/_y3PCKrRj1I2jK6BOhBUVc5K-PL?domain=garden.lovetoknow.com

SanSone, A. (2021, March 25). 15 best plants that attract pollinators: Best flowers for pollinators. The Pioneer Woman. https://url.us.m.mimecastprotect.com/s/sn6SCNkRmLS02LzE7umNhPcyoBU5?domain=thepioneerwoman.com/

The Permaculture Lab. (n.d.). Using permaculture plant guilds for low maintenance gardens. https://www.thepermaculturelab.com/blog/using-permaculture-plant-guilds-for-low-maintenance-gardens

Vinje, E. (2012, December 7). How to make your own potting soil. Planet Natural. https://url.us.m.mimecastprotect.com/s/w0e3CVO9xAhxDBY53sGQC3cEZNP4?domain=planetnatural.com/

Whittingham, J. (2012). Fruit and vegetables in pots. DK Publishing.

Witte, D. (2020, August 17). How to build nutrient-rich soil on the permaculture garden. New Life on a Homestead. Retrieved July 25, 2022, from https://www.newlifeonahomestead.com/nutrient-rich-soil-permaculture/

West Virginia University Extension. (n.d.). Companion planting. https://extension.wvu.edu/lawn-gardening-pests/gardening/garden-management/companion-planting

Zafar, S. (2020, June 5). What is vermicomposting. EcoMENA. Retrieved August 2, 2022, from https://www.ecomena.org/vermicomposting/

www.ingramcontent.com/pod-product-compliance
Lightning Source LLC
Chambersburg PA
CBHW030220100526
44584CB00014BA/1402